FEMME TYPE

CONTENTS

CONTRIBUTORS

Alice Savoie
Amy Papaelias
Ana Duje
Anastasia Liolio
Andrea Tinnes
Brooke Robinson
Caterina Bianchini
Charlotte Rohde
Erica Carras
Hello this is Kae
Hui Yeon Hwang
Imogen Ayres
Inga Plönnigs
Isabel Urbina Peña
Joana Correia
Johanne Lian Olsen
Julia Kahl
Laura Brunner
Laura Meseguer
Letitia Lin
Leonie Martin
Lilly Marques
Liron Lavi Turkenich
Lynne Yun
Maria Doreuli
María Ramos
Marina Chaccur
Marta Cerda
Marta Gawin
My Name is Wendy
Nadine Chahine
Natalie Rauch
Nuria Lopez
Pooja Saxena

Rachel Joy Price
Rita Matos
Sahar Afshar
Sandrine Nugue
Shanti Sparrow
Sibylle Hagmann
Tamara Arkatova
TienMin Liao
Tina Touli
Typelab
Verena Gerlach
Veronica Fuerte
Yarza Twins

Intro...

The concept of FEMME TYPE has been a few years in the making. The first glimpse of the idea came when I frantically scoured design books at university, soaking up as much design inspiration as I could for the projects I was undertaking. Although the internet was full of interesting online platforms that certainly had an equal amount of great content, I always turned to books as I loved the physicality of them, the bold, permanent stance that each image took on the page as part of a curated object. Therefore in reflection, FEMME TYPE is first and foremost, a product of my never-ending obsession with type and print which is why I chose to work at People of Print. Separately, I found as my eyes skimmed over the names of the designers of the beautiful work I was seeing in these books, it became quite clear that statistically there were more men than women. After a period of about two years I found myself asking: Surely there must be more women out there who are producing equally inspiring work? Why have they not been included? So I made it my mission to find them and celebrate the wonderful work that they were doing.

Pitching the idea was the easy part; what came next was a bit more challenging. Running a Kickstarter campaign is no easy feat and was uncharted territory for me. I'd like to take this opportunity to thank Marcroy Smith, without his help and mentoring this book would never have come to life, but by creating the FEMME TYPE Instagram (@femmetype) I was assured that by building a community, FEMME TYPE would surely grow and become a valuable network of creatives who share my love for type. Sure enough, with the help of our publishers People of Print and our financial patron MOO and Department Store, within three days the Kickstarter had reached its goal. Finally the cogs had been put in motion and FEMME TYPE was going to print. Not only has it been amazing to see how people are willing to support an independent project and the sense of community, but also the positive responses I received from the participants that were happy to be involved.

A final special thanks goes out to every designer who contributed to the book, in particular Leeds-based printers Pressision Ltd who partly sponsored the printing costs of the book. It's helped us produce this wonderful, affordable piece of print which I hope goes on to inspire more women and others to pursue a career in type and become a valuable educational tool for future generations to come.

Femme Type is about celebrating the work and the people. Let's see where this goes.

FEMME TYPE Founder, Curator
& Author — Amber Weaver

The 2nd Edition

I'm truly humbled to be in this position to present the 2nd edition of FEMME TYPE. After selling out in just five short months, the book, and our platform to our delight has been so well received by fellow designers and the design community. FEMME TYPE is now stocked in stores through-out the UK, Europe and and a growing amount of stores in the USA. What we can be certain of, is that we hope to continue our mission to inspire more women to pursue a career in type and to be recognised for their hard work and talent. We've got many exciting things in the woodwork and can't wait to share them with you all.

In this edition, you can find a few slight tweaks including an obvious switch up of the colours on the front cover, our new body copy typeface: Neue Kramer Grotesk which you can find in the Type Design section designed by Leonie Martin and Laura Brunner and our captions and other smaller details are set in Equitan Slab by type designer Diana Ovezea. In addition, thanks to selling out of the first print run, we've been able to invest in upping the paper weight to reduce the amount of see-through. Again all this wouldn't have been possible without our partners, our printer Pressison and not to mention our publisher Peolpe of Print (In Perpetuum). One final but necessary thanks goes out to all the Kickstarter supporters who helped bring this project to life in the first place, we wouldn't be here if it wasn't for you, so thank you!

FEMME TYPE Founder, Curator
& Author — Amber Weaver

ENJOY

FOREWORD

Bike riding along the West Coast of the United States
from Vancouver to the border of Mexico was where my
love of letters was ignited. What I saw was a treasure trove
of type, lettering, hand painted murals and huge lettered
logos and luminous signs all of which littered my journey
and henceforth began my journey of Goodtype. Goodtype
is primarily an Instagram platform showcasing an online
community of lettering artists from around the world.
Having practised design for nearly a decade, I was always
drawn to letter forms and soon after launching Goodtype,
I realised I was not alone in this love and admiration for the
letter arts. The Goodtype community grew very quickly and I
was astonished by how many people shared my admiration.
As I watched, this art form unified hundreds of thousands of
people across the globe and I posed the question, why?
Why is this art form so popular and how does it connect
with such a diverse and wide audience? The letter arts a
llows us as creatives to boundlessly express ourselves
within a specific message. A viewer may not necessarily
relate to the message but could be drawn to the artistic style
 of the way it's represented. It could say anything and they
could somehow still connect with the style the letter forms

take within a space. Or vice versa, the viewer might not necessarily connect with the letter forms, but could relate to the specific message displayed. Written language is our most vital method of human communication. The written language paired with art and design is a key combination that has proven to connect humans from all reaches of the globe.

Once these connections had been made, micro-communities began to organise themselves around this art form. Inspired by the largely supportive community that began to grow on Instagram, I began diving into the relationships and positive interactions that were being cultivated. The letter arts combined with social media created a space for designers to come together and discover each other's talents and potential. It allowed us to discover new and up and coming designers as well as female designers that have helped shape the direction of the letter arts. As a graphic designer, artist and curator, my passion for type still bleeds into everything I do. I've discovered so many wonderful women art communities such as Women of Type, Women of Illustration and Ladies Who Paint and by discovering FEMME TYPE, we can continue to construct valuable sources of inspiration and education for future and current designers.

Several years ago when I first began my hunt for type, I observed type design was quite a male dominated territory. It didn't seem like a space where many women were actively contributing. Or perhaps women were, but not being seen or recognised. I believe that social media had a massive impact in terms of opening our eyes to the possibilities of type design and it showed us, along with everything else, that it is a space for equality. It inspired us to find each other, come together and celebrate one another and over the years, I have seen the type industry grow and develop into a brilliant space now hosting a sea of talented people from all walks of life. The letter arts combined with social media will always ebb and flow in trends and styles and since 2013, I've seen the popularity in hand lettering explode, fragmenting into many different genres and styles. FEMME TYPE does a beautiful job at showcasing type in all its forms, celebrating highly skilled women on an international level. Which is why I am so very honoured to be writing the foreword for FEMME TYPE's first print publication. Thank you FEMME TYPE for creating this platform and giving a voice to the many female type and lettering artists around the world and also giving us the opportunity to be properly recognised. Thank you, Amber Weaver and People of Print, for making the effort of creating such a beautiful, informative and diverse print publication.

– Brooke Robinson, Chief Curator and Founder of Goodtype

ESSAY 01

MARÍA RAMOS

Alphabettes contributor &
co-founder of NM Type.

Typewriter Typefaces and their Influence on Digital Fonts

Think about typewriters for a minute. What comes to your mind? You may be hearing the sound of the keyboard or perhaps imagining some simple printed text. What's for sure, is that the term typewriter transports us back to another moment in time. Even today, when it's connected to something new, there's a certain nostalgia attached to it. The typewriter was invented in the 19th century to allow people to print documents in an easy and immediate manner. The first models manufactured had significant limitations as they only used uppercase letters and the text was not visible while typing. Those initial constraints would be overcome on future models, as manufacturers felt compelled to respond to users' needs and make more functional and efficient machines. From mechanical to electronic models, several innovations were introduced. While mechanical models only used one monospaced font per machine, the electric and electronic typewriters allowed the use of several fonts and offered typefaces with different character widths. It's then easy to understand why monospaced and typewriter in digital fonts are not always exchangeable terms, as not all typefaces created for the machine were monospaced.

The complex combinations of keys we use today in computers did not exist for typewriters. The keyboard included a lever to activate caps and each key was connected to only two characters. Manufacturers had to be inventive to fit all the characters needed in a particular language onto a very limited keyboard. This was one of the reasons for the particular shapes of some typewriter characters. There were designs that had to serve different purposes. The straight form of the quotation mark, for example, was either placed at the beginning or the end of a quote. It could also be part of certain composed characters such as the exclamation mark and the dieresis.

There were other characters that adopted peculiar shapes in order to meet the requirements of the typewriter. Type designers worked within the limitations of the machine, especially in mechanical models. Some design features were used to improve the irregular rhythm created by monospaced characters. The lower middle joint in the 'w', the 'J' sitting on

FF Trixie Heavy
FF Trixie Rough Heavy
FF Trixie HD Heavy

American Typewriter ITC Pro Medium

Adobe Courier Std Medium

Lettera Regular & Candia

Valentine & Quadratto

IBM Plex Mono Regular Italic

Pitch and Pitch Sans Regular

Operator Book and Book Italic

Vulf Mono Regular and Italic

Type samples of digital typefaces inspired by
typewriter letterforms. Courtesy of María Ramos.

the baseline, or the missing serifs in the 'm' are just a few examples
of new conventions in typewriter type design. All these details were
decisions made by the designers so the printed text had a better
appearance. The low printing quality of the machine was also very
relevant for the design. Typewriters used a transfer method for printing.
The metal type bars in mechanical models hit the roller through a ribbon,
leaving a mark on the paper. The final appearance of the text depended
on several factors: the pressure applied to the keys, the amount of ink in
the ribbon, the condition of the type slugs, etc. This all resulted in an
irregular text colour on the printed page. The electric and electronic
models introduced a system that controlled the striking force of the
type on paper, obtaining a more uniform printed page. Another factor
was the material of the ribbon. Cotton, silk and nylon were some of the

fabrics used in the industry. Comparing the results of different ribbons, it turns out that those made of polythene (a plastic material) achieve clearer printed outlines for the characters. All these limiting conditions of the machine should help us understand the reasons for the particular forms in typewriter typefaces. These new shapes would become a reference for many digital designers. Today, without the limitations of the machine, some of those designs are still available in our devices. There are many examples of the so-called "typewriter typefaces" in the digital industry, although doubts arise around the definition of this term. Many type styles included in conventional classifications were also designs created for typewriters. I would say "typewriter" is not a style, but a term used to convey an idea behind a particular design. Within all the typefaces included in this category, there are different approaches to the term. Some fonts use a real typewriter typeface as an influence for a digital design. Others try to mimic the appearance of typewritten documents and both can be considered digital typewriter fonts.

For a better definition of this genre, we will mention some typefaces that can serve as an example. Included in the designs that try to recreate the appearance of typewritten texts, we find FF Trixie. It was first released in 1991 and would rapidly become a favourite for mystery and intrigue films and series. It seems the designer, Erik van Blokland, was not entirely satisfied with his first design. Early printing and operating systems could just handle a limited number of points, so he had to simplify the design. However, with the arrival of OpenType technology, the type family was expanded to include more refined outlines and alternative shapes. The new additions to the family created a more convincing design, which better replicated the appearance of a real typewritten text. Among the first digital typewriter typefaces we should mention a classic, American Typewriter. Originally designed for phototypesetting, it was created by Joel Kaden and Tony Stan in 1974. The distorted outlines on the design were used in phototype printing for the ink to reach the contours of the characters. This same trick could have been used in typewriters for a sharper appearance of the text. American Typewriter has a clear connection to the early typefaces created for the machine, but the design was not restricted to a monospaced treatment. As stated in a specimen from 1975, "American Typewriter strikes a happy compromise with its forerunner. The rigid spacing is dispensed with, but the distinctive properties of
the typewriter face is generously enhanced."

There are also some typefaces that were originally created for typewriters and adapted later to the digital format. Amongst these, Courier is the most popular. Howard Kettler designed it in 1955 for IBM machines and the company introduced the font into the market as a fresh, crisp and modern new typewriter face. There are so many different digital versions of Courier that it would be difficult to choose which one is most faithful to the original. Courier was extensively used as a default option for computers and printers, and it became a standard for screenplays and coding. It is always hard to discover the underlying reasons for the success of a font. While comparing Courier to other typefaces previously used in the machine we can spot some clear differences. Taking the Olivetti typeface that inspired Typewriter (Henrik Kubel, 2012) as a reference, there is a rational design approach to Courier which avoids ball terminals and dismisses some curved strokes and complex forms like the double storey 'g'. Courier could be considered a modern update of those first typefaces connected to the machine for many decades.

Other digital typewriter fonts are based on rare typefaces not so popular at the time. The font library of Lineto includes some good examples of this. Valentine (Stephan Müller, 2002) is an interpretation of the typeface Quadratto that Arturo Rolfo originally designed for the Olivetti Valentine. Inspired by Eurostile and Microgamma, Quadratto belonged to a particular typewriter style, techno/cubic. Another example, Lettera, could be included on the list of successful digital typewriter typefaces. Created by Kobi Benezni in 2006, his design was based on Candia, a typeface that Josef Müller-Brockmann created for Olivetti in the 70s. This digital design was very popular in the market and users asked for a proportional version. Lettera-Txt was born in 2012. It's interesting to see how all these typefaces, based on original designs for typewriters, became type families. The typefaces created for the machine were actually single fonts, and the idea of a type family was quite different from now. In their interpretation of a typewriter typeface, designers had to adapt the original design to different weights and styles.

Real typewriter typefaces are also found as a reference in large type systems. These are super type families where the design is adapted to different type genres. The custom fonts in IBM Plex (2017), for example, used original samples from the company to develop the monospaced Italic cut. New contemporary interpretations of typewriter ideas include typefaces like Pitch (2012, 2018) by Kris Sowersby, Operator (2016) by Andy Clymer, and Vulf Mono (2016) by James Edmondson. There are many more examples that could be mentioned and many more to come, but the purpose of this article is not to create an extensive list. The main aim of this text is to show, especially for those who have never used a typewriter, where we can find the influence of the machine in our digital fonts. The truth is that those peculiar letter shapes originally created for the typewriter are very much alive today. Many designers feel inspired by the creative solutions proposed to mitigate the technical limitations of old machines. The typewriter played an important role in many offices and homes for more than 100 years, and also left its imprint on the history of type. It pushed the development of our alphabets and made us rethink how we shape them.

ESSAY 02

TienMin Liao

Designer and typographer specialising in
letterforms and logotype Kanji/Chinese.

Bilingual Lettering

In 2016, I began a series of Latin-Kanji pairing studies titled "Bilingual Lettering". This project documents over fifty pairing exercises as well as thoughts and notes gained throughout the process. These pairing examples are not solutions for developing systematic typefaces, rather the results of customising the word 'TYPE (type)' and '字' (1). Since both writing systems have very different character structures and are traditionally written using different tools, flexibility is necessary in order to inject the same personality into both scripts. Each bilingual lettering pair is a custom result, so there isn't only one solution. The lettering discussed here highlights pairs that express brand personality equally in both languages, rather than one playing the hero while the other plays a supportive role.

(1) In order to make a fair comparison between each exercise, only use 'TYPE (type)' and '字' as specimen. Some expressional forms such as lowercase 'g' or 'na' (捺) unfortunately cannot be taken into consideration.

The process of this experiment is divided into four sections: Observation, Making, Consistency and Alternatives. The most important criteria for designing bilingual lettering with legibility and basic type knowledge in mind is whether or not it's able to express a similar personality in both scripts, as opposed to simply sharing a similar appearance.

1. Observation
There are naturally vast differences of contour, density and form between Latin and Kanji. In Latin script, a word is composed with the 26-letter alphabet arranged from left to right whilst the other contains the contour of a word which can be viewed as a horizontal rectangular shape, and most strokes go vertically rather than horizontally with similar thickness. The negative spaces between the strokes are also visually equivalent. Overall, the texture of Latin script is in most cases pretty even and carries no meanings. Although it's also composed with small units, Kanji, on the other hand, is completely different. With its complex composition, some characters are constituted within a single unit and some within multiple units. Some characters are assembled with just a few strokes while others may go up to twenty or more. Unlike Latin script, the stroke thickness in Kanji varies from one to another, depending on its structure and the number of strokes.

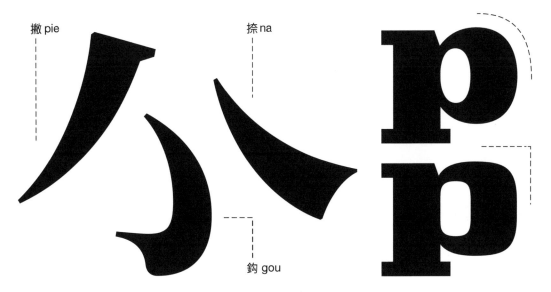

Figure (c)

Although they are drawn within squares, the actual character contour is not always a square. It can be a triangle like '森', a diamond shape like '今', or a vertical rectangle like '目'. A word/phrase is usually made up of one to three (or more) Kanji, which makes the word contour even more complex. The differences in the density, shapes and visual rhythm of Kanji makes it challenging to create bilingual letterings. In addition to the overall construction, their stroke direction is also distinctly different. The amount of vertical strokes in Kanji is usually more than the horizontal ones and there are no real circular

Figure (e)

strokes ('撇', '捺' and '鈎' have strokes that are only slightly "curvy" (ⓒ). In contrast, nearly half of the Latin alphabet contains round shapes. Some are even close to a fully circular shape, especially 'O', 'Q', 'C', '0', 'b', 'd', 'p' and 'q'. How these round shapes are designed is one of the key factors of type personality. For instance, making the round shapes more squarish will drastically alter the type personality, but this factor doesn't apply in Kanji since most of its strokes are relatively straight. The structural differences discussed above are a key challenge in the development of bilingual letterings. It is essential to have a basic typographic knowledge of both languages such as configuration, proportion, optical correction and so on. For example, the four squares in character '東' are all different sizes and the 'O' is usually taller and lower than 'I'. This is called an overshoot ⓔ. Since Latin and Kanji scripts are traditionally drawn with different tools, graphic designers tend to apply the traits from one script to the other directly without considering the fundamental rules of foreign type.

Figure (e)

(2) 漢字 (simplified Chinese: 汉字) is pronounced differently in many languages, such as Hanzi in Mandarin, Hanji in Taiwanese, and Kanji in Japanese, but they all refer to the same writing system that's widely used in East Asia and originated from China. The traditional version is used in Taiwan and Hong Kong while the simplified version is adopted in Mainland China. 漢字 is also used in Japanese along with their syllabary, hiragana and katakana. In this essay, "Kanji" is used to refer to 漢字 since it is already widely known in English.

2. Making
There is never only one approach to create a bilingual lettering. Depending on the design object and design intent, solutions can be hugely different. Existing type genres can be paired or brand new styles can be created to match each other. The most important thing to keep in mind throughout the design process is that both scripts should convey the same message and personality rather than being limited to only sharing similar appearances. What's the meaning that this logotype/lettering wants to convey? Can this logotype/lettering express the spirit of the design object (client/brand)? Here are some approaches to create bilingual letterings.

Approach 1: Pairing with the existing type genre
Certain Kanji typeface genres are commonly associated with serif and sans-serif typefaces. In most cases, Ming-ti (明體 / JP: Mincho-tai), is considered a similar genre to serif typefaces, while Hei-ti (黑體 / JP: goshikku-tai) is viewed as sans-serif. (3) It's relatively easy to create a bilingual lettering within these two kinds of type genre as long as we make sure their visual parameters are consistent (such as concentration, balance, visual centre, contrast, texture, details and so on; see "Consistency" for more detail.) In addition to Ming-ti and Hei-ti, serif and sans-serif, there are some calligraphic

scripts that can't be directly associated with any scripts in another language, such as Blackletter, italic, Cao-shu (草書) and Li-shu (隸書). These are traditionally drawn with distinct writing tools with specific rules. While it's not always necessary to match appearances, the two languages do need to have the same personality. So how can this be achieved? It depends on the design objective. Take the Blackletter as an example: if the assignment is to create a Kanji logotype to pair with a Blackletter newspaper masthead, the Kanji has to demonstrate a sense of authority. Stylising Kanji to mimic Blackletter may cause it to lose the seriousness of a masthead, but choosing a script that exhibits "classic" and "trustful," such as high-contrast Ming-ti can be a great solution. The New York Times Chinese masthead designed by Julius Hui is a great example. (4) However, when the style of the Blackletter is used for a different design intent, such as a heavy metal band, a Blackletter-stylised Kanji design can enhance the visual impact.

Approach 2: Coordinating styles

For a brand/design subject with a stronger personality, rather than pairing the existing type, we can create a new style as long as we don't lose legibility or its basic skeleton. Here are a few different approaches to coordinating styles.

A. Using the features as decorative elements

In this approach, we can extract traits (such as stroke end-shape, serif style, etc.) as a decorative element and transfer them onto the other script without making any weight-distribution and structural changes ⓕ. To compare, take Approach 1's Blackletter as an example again. Now we already have Ming-ti as a base-structure and then try to bring features from Blackletter into Ming-ti. If we try to carry the curve from Blackletter onto Ming-ti, it will make it look very unnatural since it's traditionally carved on wood and the strokes in Ming-ti are mostly straight and barely curved. However, we can make Ming-ti look more Blackletter-like if we replace Ming-ti's triangle shape with the unique diamond shape from Blackletter as an additional decorative element.

B. Imagine drawing with the same tools

In addition to treating the traits as decorative elements, another way to stylise the type is to imagine using the same tools to create both scripts. This approach would be a great solution for calligraphic or brush-drawn type and will allow both scripts to share a more similar appearance. However, this kind of non-traditional drawing may deviate from traditional weight distribution and make the type look informal or over-stylised. There are some aspects to consider while creating bilingual lettering with this approach: what kind of material is the tool made of? If it is a brush, how hard is the brush? At what angle is the pen held? How thick is the ink? How rough is the paper? What kind of personality does the writer/painter have? With these considerations in mind, imagine using the same tools, gestures, speed, movements, etc. to draw the two scripts rather than copying the strokes onto the other type. Because of structural differences, there is no way to have the exact same drawing ⑨.

C. Treat it as a graphic

If the objective is to create a more expressive lettering, other than working within existing type categories, we can also treat the type as a graphic. With an illustrative approach like this, the biggest consideration is legibility. It is crucial to make sure all the letters are distinguished from one another. As for Kanji, the recognisability of the form is more important than the clarity of each individual stroke since native users identify characters based on contour of both radicals (units) and their complete form rather than stroke structure.

(3) Although they share some similarities in appearance which make them easy to pair, they are not equivalent to each other.

(4) "Typography 02" (Taiwan) 2016, page 30–33, Print. ; Type is beautiful: 記紐約時報》中文牌匾設計

(5) There is usually a triangle shape on every horizontal stroke in Ming-ti. Sometimes this is considered "serif" when compared to western typography.

Broad edge pen

Figure (f)

3. Consistency

After sketching out a style with the approaches above, the next step is to make sure that all the visual parameters are consistent, which may include: colour, concentration, balance, tension, visual centre, contrast, details and overall impression lockup, etc.

1. Colour

The "colour" here refers to overall proportion of the positive and negative spaces rather than any actual colour. As most Kanji characters are more complicated and denser than Latin script, Kanji would usually be made a little bit bigger and lighter, so the amount of "ink" will be the same. If the two languages were made with the same colour, it would make the Kanji look too heavy.

2. Expansion and contraction

There is no such thing as x-height in Kanji , but "中宮" ("Centre Space") can be viewed as a similar concept. Latin alphabets are constructed vertically with three layers, one on top of another divided by x-height and baseline, while every Kanji is constructed as a two-dimensional layout. "Centre Space" literally means the centre box in a 3X3 metric, and the size of this centre box will decide how modern the type looks. We can view "Centre Space" as a x-height with two axes. Similar to x-height, a Kanji with contracted "Centre Space" usually gives a more traditional impression, while expansive "Centre Space" looks more modern. However, unlike x-height, the size of "Centre Space" is completely perceptional, and can't be measured with specific values.

3. Tension and balance

When Kanji and Latin characters are set together, there is tension between their negative space. The tension between each character must be equal to the balance of the word.

4. Visual centre

The visual centre of the two languages should proportionally be of the same height. If we consider each Kanji as a two-dimensional image, we can find a visual centre in each character, while the visual centre of a Latin type is decided by the horizontal stroke design. Most of the horizontal strokes of Latin alphabets fall onto the Cap height, x-height and baseline, so the design of those two-storey letters, such as 'A', 'B', 'E', 'F', 'G', 'H', 'P', 'R', 'S', 'X', 'Y' and 'a', 'e', 'g', 's', 'x', are key to deciding where the visual centre falls.

Figure (k)

5. Contrast

The contrast of thick and thin strokes should be consistent between both scripts.

6. Details

When we pair Kanji and Latin characters, we can carry details from one to the other, such as the angle of cut, serif, terminal shapes and so on ⓚ.

7. Material and overall impression

In terms of the consistency of the material, in addition to imagining the type drawn with the same tool as mentioned above, we can also consider the idea of material as an abstract concept, such as "plumpness". For instance, think about how much air is inside this type? The overall impression can be tough, warm or full ①.

Figure (m)

8. Lock-up or individual version

Two scripts can be locked-up together or used as two individual versions of lettering depending on the marketing strategy. When two scripts are locked-up, we need to adjust the relationship between them to maintain balance.

4. Alternatives

When creating bilingual lettering, the form of the translation may match the other script perfectly, but sometimes they don't share anything in common visually. The best scenario is to take the letter form into consideration during the naming stage. If the translation can't be altered, we can also look for other forms as an alternative solution.

Naming

As mentioned in the observation section, the density of a Kanji character varies from a few strokes to sometimes more than twenty. The differences in density create a visual rhythm in paragraphs, but when creating a logotype/lettering with a few characters, it may become problematic and off-balanced.

Forms

The last and final section is form. If the translation can't be changed, another solution would be to look for alternative forms. For example, in Latin, should we be using a single-storey 'g' or double-storey 'g'? Connected 'y' or two-stroke 'y'? The same is true for Kanji: we can look up alternative forms in vintage books, handwriting styles, or reference forms from other Kanji-using countries.(6) We can also alter or simplify the form as long as the type is legible and aesthetically pleasing Ⓜ.

(6) For example, the first stroke of '字' can be drawn as a point, but can also be written as a short vertical stroke.

This experiment in Kanji-Latin pairings reveals a range of approaches to solve bilingual lettering. Even when - as in this case - there are vast differences between writing systems, a flexible and explorative approach helps to create lettering where brand style or personality can be fully expressed in both.

TYPE DESIGN

Johanne Lian Olsen
Andrea Tinnes
Leonie Martin &
Laura Brunner
Imogen Ayres
Nuria Lopez
Verena Gerlach
Typelab
Sibylle Hagmann
Amy Papaelias
Laura Meseguer
Natalie Rauch
Pooja Saxena
Nadine Chahine
Maria Doreuli
TienMin Liao
Lilly Marques
Charlotte Rohde
Rachel Joy Price
Ana Duje
Joana Correia
Inga Plönnigs
Sandrine Nugue
Alice Savoie
Erica Carras
Julia Kahl
Liron Lavi Turkenich
Lynne Yun

Johanne Lian Olsen is a Norwegian graphic designer working in the areas of type design, editorial design and illustration. Some of Johanne's clients include IKEA, NIKE and The Unseen to name a few, as she continues to focus on both print and digital media from initial concept development right through to art-working in both type design and typography.

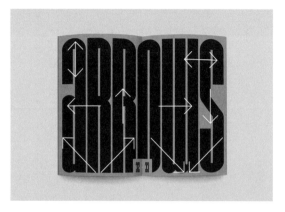

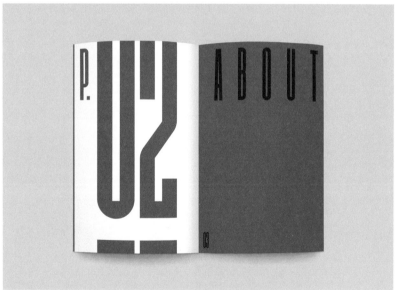

Due Display was made in early 2017 as a parting gift to a former employer (Studio Claus Due). The font consists of 4 cuts/weights and was designed to look as tall and thin as the man himself. **Due Display** has a bold stance offering an alternative italic style to its regular original.

@j_lianolsen
www.lianolsen.com

ABC—äã

DUE DISPLAY •

A B C D E F G H I J K L M N O P

a b c d e f g h i j k l m n o p

NO. 0123456789

. - - - - - - - - - -

CONDENSED/SLIM

ABC — ∂ää ¶

DUE DISPLAY •

A B C D E F G H I J K L M N O P R S T U V W X Y Z

a b c d e f g h i j k l m n o p r s t u v w x y z

TRONDHEIM NO
DK COPENHAGEN.
LONDON GB
GB SWANSEA.

08:06:19

WORK

17:34:02

PLAY

NIKE

Typeface
Nike Football Font
(2017)

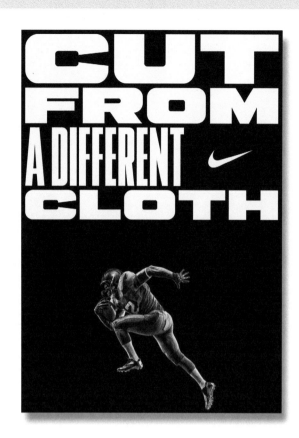

IT'S NOT WHERE THEY TAKE YOU,
IT'S WHERE YOU TAKE THEM.
STRONGER, FASTER AND TOGETHER.
FORWARD. LEAVE NOTHING.
THIS IS YOUR STAGE.
OWN THE SUMMER.
GAME CHANGER. ALL IN.

hellö

UPPER CASE
ABCDEFGHIJKLMNOPQR
STUVWXYZ
ÀÁÄÅÈÉËÆÒÓÖØÙÚÜ

LOWER CASE
abcdefghijklmnopqrstuvwxyz
àáäåæèéëòóöøùúü

NUMBERS
1234567890

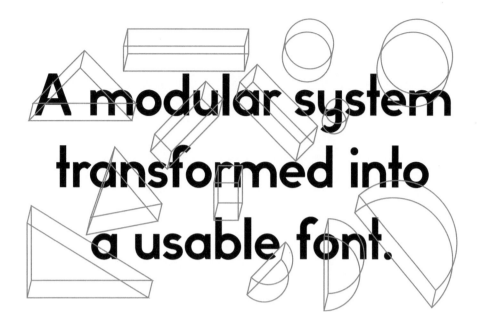

A modular system transformed into a usable font.

Typeface
Infant (2014)

Having designed several well constructed typefaces, in 2014 Johanne added another beautiful font to the list. **Infant Display** was designed as a part of an educational kit helping children understand the construction of letters. The kit also contains physical building blocks to help teach and understand how letters are formed by allowing them to build them themselves. **Infant Display** is designed from basic shapes found in the building blocks where the proportions are consistent, as the relation between a letter's appearance, its meaning and what it sounds like can be hard to grasp for a child learning to read and write. The outcome is a legible font where the separate letters are easy to distinguish from each other. **Infant Display** is a clear, simple, yet playful font with additional children's books with texts connecting stories to how the alphabet is shaped.

Infant

Featured in the likes of Eye Magazine and TYPO Talks, esteemed graphic and type designer Andrea Tinnes produces cutting edge fonts with a brilliant series of innovative type families. Based in Berlin, Andrea combines her talents of teaching, identity design and type, applying it to the work which makes up her impressive portfolio.

Library of Shapes, Texts and
Structures Exhibition
Typeface: Affiche (2019)

@andrea.tinnes
www.typecuts.com

LIBRARY OF SHAPES TEXTS AND STRUCTURES

AFFICHE

AFFICHE

CAPS ONLY
DISPLAY FAMILY
FOR POSTERS

HEADLINE

AFFICHE

3 WIDTHS

3 SANS STYLES
3 WIDDDTHS
3 SERIF STYLES

SANS & SERIF
VERSIONS
REVERSEIT

+12° ITALICS
−12° REVERSE
ITALICS

AFH

+19°

TYPE
FACE

CHE

PLUSSS

ALTERRRNATES

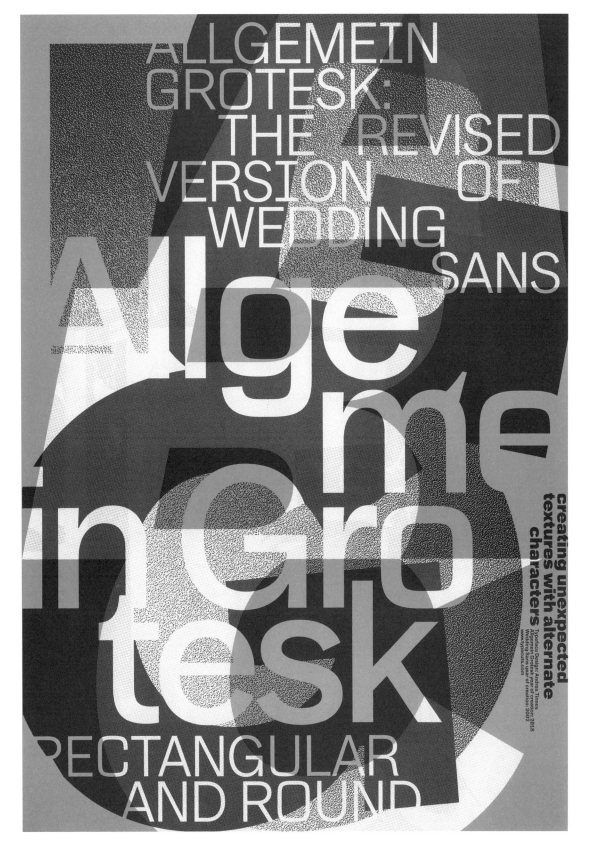

ALLGEMEIN GROTESK: THE REVISED VERSION OF WEDDING SANS

Allgemeine Grotesk

RECTANGULAR AND ROUND

creating unexpected
textures with alternate
characters

Typeface Design: Andrea Tinnes
Allgemein Grotesk year of creation: 2018
Wedding Sans year of creation: 2002
www.typecuts.com

ABCCCCCD
ABCDEFGH
EFGHIJKLM
IJKLMNOOO
NOPQRRR
PQRRRRSSS
SSSTUVW
TUVWXYZ
XYZ123123

AFFICHE

ANNICHE

CAPS ONLY
DISPLAY FAMILY
FOR POSTERS

HEADLINE

3 WIDTHS

3 SANS STYLES
3 WIDDDTHS
3 SERIF STYLES

SANS & SERIF

VERSIONS

REVERSEIT

+12° ITALICS
−12° REVERSE
ITALICS

CHE

+19°

TYPE

FACE

PLUSSS

ALTERRRNATES

ALLGEMEIN GROTESK: THE REVISED VERSION OF WEDDING SANS

Allgemein Grotesk

MIXING ROUND AND SQUARE

forms into one single typeface via opentype features

Typeface Design: Andrea Tinnes
Allgemein Grotesk, revised version of
Wedding Sans year of creation: 2002
www.typecuts.com

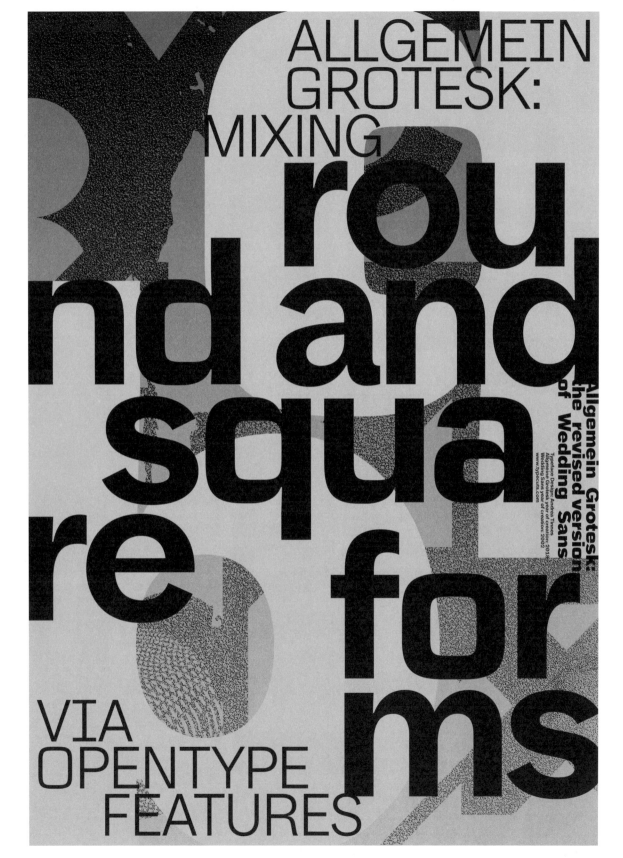

ALLGEMEIN GROTESK: MIXING round and square forms VIA OPENTYPE FEATURES

Allgemein Grotesk:
the revised version
of Wedding Sans

Typeface Design: Andrea Tinnes
Allgemein Grotesk year of creation: 2018
Wedding Sans year of creation: 2002
www.typecuts.com

AFFICHE

P.LUSSS

+12°

HEADLINE

& TYPEFACE'N'

TYPEFACE'N'

WIDTHS

3 WIDTHS

3 SANS

3

SERIF

+12° CAPS ONLY

CAPS ONLY

CAPS ONLY
DISPLAY FAMILY
FOR POSTERS

+12° ITALICS
-12° REVERSE
ITALICS

MANY

NEW

Project examples of Andrea's bold style include **Affiche** and **Allgemein Grotesk**. **Affiche** is an all caps multiple width display family and was conceived as a highly versatile typographic instrument. **Affiche** includes 3 distinct serif styles such as Romana, Latin and Stencil as well as 3 sans variants, distinguished by their terminals on curved strokes (diagonal, horizontal and vertical terminal cuts). Each capital comes in 3 finely adjusted widths: condensed, narrow and normal, distributed over uppercase, lowercase and small caps positions. The various widths can be used separately or manually mixed, providing many variations in colour and texture. In addition, **Affiche** challenges the user with its many stylistics sets, including alternate glyphs for characters such as 'O', 'Q', 'C', 'D' and 'G' (round forms), 'I', 'J', 'K', 'M', 'R' and 'W' as well as stylistic alternates for several figures and punctuation. Each font contains a variety of special characters (e.g. Capital Eszett, Interrobang and Arrows), geometrical symbols and ornaments. Diacritics are compact for tight line spacing with additional alter-nates for 'Ä', 'Ö' and 'Ü'. Finally, each style offers matching italics and reverse italics (Slant: + 12° and – 12°). The first release includes one single weight per style and more weights will be added further on in the future.

    Allgemein Grotesk (2018) is the revised version of Wedding Sans (2002). Similar to **Wedding Sans**, **Allgemein Grotesk** (meaning "Generic Grotesk") explores the idea of adding an unexpected twist and personality to a seemingly ordinary sans-serif typeface by combining round and square letter forms. The alternate square characters such as e.g. 'O', 'C', 'D', 'G', 'U', 'a', 'o', 'c', 'd', 'e', 'g', 'h', 'n', 'o', 'u', figures, etc. can all be separately switched on, allowing the user to twist and control the overall tone of the typeface.

    Other characteristics are the increasingly wider proportions throughout the various weights as well as the r light punctuations such as dashes, bars, slashes, brackets, etc. **Allgemein Grotesk** currently features six weights — light, regular, medium, bold, extrabold and super — as well as a bold condensed and a regular monospaced version. Each project and its fonts include many of Andrea's bold typographical layouts showcasing the powerful letter forms and varied weights as well as geometric symbols and arrows. The images showcase a series of experimental typographic posters featuring the **Affiche** and **Allgemein Grotesk** from the designers latest exhibition at the A-Z space in Berlin, Germany.

Creative design duo Leonie & Laura
are Berlin-based type designers who
have produced several fonts including
their geometric sans-serif type family
Neue Kramer Grotesk. As part of
Klingspor Institute of Type Design, a
cooperation between HfG Offenbach
and Klingspor Museum, they're working
on building a connection between the
past and the present of type design in
the city of Offenbach.

NKG Type Specimen
NKG Text 90 (2017)

www.turbo-type.com
www.klingspor-institute.com

Neue Kramer Grotesk is a geometric sans-serif based on a sketch of a capital alphabet from the early 1920s dedicated to architect Ferdinand Kramer. In addition, **Neue Kramer Grotesk** is a multiple master font containing five weights in two different styles. Text is optimised for smaller sizes and good readability whilst Display offers a wide range of various alternative glyphs. Designed digitally, **NKG** has a certain notion of fluidity and motion while being static and geometric. Inspired by Kramer's approaches, this monolinear typeface combines modern technology and a contemporary, clear appearance with an architectural essence of simplicity and construction. It captures the slightly odd singularity of the early sketch of so-called **Kramer Grotesk.**

Neue Kramer Grotesk Display

Neue Kramer Grotesk Display

Neue Kramer Grotesk Display

Neue Kramer Grotesk Display

Neue Kramer Grotesk Display

Neue Kramer Grotesk Text

Neue Kramer Grotesk Text

Neue Kramer Grotesk Text

Neue Kramer Grotesk Text

LEONIE MARTIN & LAURA BRUNNER

005

ÁĂĂĂÂÂÄÀĀĄÅ
ÅÃÆÆ

!¡?¿&'"()*

óŏŏôöòőō
øǿõœ

abcdefghijklmnopqrstu
vwxyz

220pt

Ligatures

Ex- Communications Design student Imogen Ayres founded her own type foundry. After working on collaborative projects at Glasgow-based company Paulin, Imogen took the plunge into launching her own type foundry, aiming to create instinct-led typefaces with unique conceptual starting points.

Typeface
Zetkin (2018)

@mobeltype
www.mobeltype.com

ABCDEF
GHIJKLM
NOPQRST
UVWXYZ
".,?!&----"
1234567890

Typeface
Do you Dance? (2018)

Möbel Type Foundry began in the summer after Imogen graduated from her Communication Design course at the **Glasgow School of Art**. She specialised in graphic design and began experimenting with type design as a relief from a research heavy project in her final year. Following graduation Imogen spent time doing freelance type design commissions as well as working for Glasgow-based company **Paulin**. At **Paulin** Imogen worked collaboratively on various products, including watches, leather goods and homewares, as well as bespoke type for watch and clock faces. One of Imogen's most recent commissions was working on a brief for **Kellenberger–White**, a studio based London which specialises in playful and process-led design work with a focus on typography.

ABCDE
GHIJK
NOPQI
VWXY

EF - —

KLM- —

RSTU —

Z!@

Typeface
Zonophone
(2018)

Spanish designer Nuria Lopez is a freelance graphic designer who lives in Jerez. Nuria specialises in branding, typography design, and the use of design as a tool for building a project with a strong social charge, influence and impact. She believes that design must have a stronger role in our society in order to change the world we currently live in.

Cuerpos que se miran
Type Design (2017)

Blind Words
Type Design
(2016)

Verena Gerlach is a Germany-based type designer who founded her own Berlin-based studio back in 1998. Since 2006 Verena has been working as a freelance book designer for art book publishers such as Hatje Cantz and Kerber Verlag.

FF Sizmo (2017)

The inspiration for **Sizmo** was found on a GDR (DDR) tenants' index board, on which movable white plastic capital letters were fixed by a thick line to the wooden board. This line is an important part of the font's appearance but there is also a variant without the line, which shows how the letters appeared when fixed behind a thin bar on the board. In 2006, the **Hochschule der Künste Bern (HKB)** commissioned Verena to design the missing lowercase letters, to be used for the signage system, cut into metal.

FF Karbid (2011)

FF Karbid (1999) was originally inspired by a German storefront lettering from the 1930s. Using this as her inspiration, Verena then disseminated its spirit into a family of well-behaved but energetic text faces. In 2011, the typeface was redesigned and extended: it now has ten basic styles plus Text, Slab and Display versions. **FF Karbid Pro Display** kept most of the peculiarities of the inspiring storefront. **FF Karbid Pro Text** reveals a simplified, more neutral design while FF Karbid Pro Slab is a completely new companion. All families contain Light, Regular, Medium, Bold, Black and their Italics. Many alternate characters have been added, for example low- and high-waist uppercase letter versions in **Karbid Pro**, **FF Karbid Pro Text** and **FF Karbid Pro Slab**; single-storey 'a' and 'g' as well as bullets and arrows. All versions of **FF Karbid Pro** contain numerous alternate characters, so that each typeface can considerably change its overall appearance. These alternates are based on Art Deco letterings with their sometimes rather eccentric shapes.

@vgerlach
www.fraugerlach.de

Karbid Display Pro Black
Karbid Display Pro Black Italic
Karbid Display Pro Bold
Karbid Display Pro Bold Italic
Karbid Display Pro Medium
Karbid Display Pro Medium Italic
Karbid Display Pro Regular
Karbid Display Pro Italic
Karbid Display Pro Light Italic
Karbid Display Pro Light

Sizmo Bold
Sizmo Bold Oblique
Sizmo Demi Bold
Sizmo Demi Bold Oblique
Sizmo Medium
Sizmo Medium Oblique
Sizmo Oblique
Sizmo Regular
Sizmo Light Oblique
Sizmo Light

ABCDEFGHIJ
KLMNOPQRST
UVWXYZ

a à á â ã ä å æ ē ĕ ė è
é ê ë ì í î ï ī ĩ ò ó ô õ
ö ù ú û ü ū ŭ ů

1234567890!
@ £ $ % ^ & * ( ) : ?

 » — · ≠ › ‹ ™

à à ă â

ã ä å æ

ē ĕ ė è

VERENA GERLACH

008

TYPELAB

Typelab is a digital platform founded by French type designer Floriane Rousselot. **Typelab's** online resource first and foremost aims to showcase typefaces from young designers and students through a system of curation. The second function, which is essential to **Typelab**, is to create a link between the different designers building a sort of community, which can encourage future projects and collaborations.

How was Typelab formed?

The idea developed during my last year whilst I was completing my Masters degree a year or so ago. Some of my friends were designing new, interesting typefaces and it all basically started from there. I had some typefaces myself too but struggled to get them featured in foundries or other distributors' websites. From this struggle, I decided to create my own platform to promote my friends' work and my own. As it naturally grew, I started to reach out to other type designers in a similar situation as me and invited them to be featured on **Typelab**.

What are your typeface designs influenced by?

My own typefaces are informed by contextual influences. My **Galejade** typeface was influenced by the city of Marseille. The culture, the people, the graphic shapes I would find in the streets, the history and many other things I saw were the subject of my analysis, with **Galejade** being the visual answer to that. In the future I would like to develop this process to create typefaces which could be the representation of other cities and cultures - a typographic anthropology, if you will. The other typefaces I designed are more based on unclear influences that I couldn't pinpoint, to be honest. It can be looking at a friend's work, or a visual representation of music projects. Mainly, the way people are living and communicating are the basis of my type projects.

What sorts of typefaces have you designed?

Mainly lettering and figurative typefaces. I used to work through graphic shapes to construct my letters and I wanted to promote figurative typefaces on **Typelab**, which are playful and experimental. Making it easy to see where the designer wanted to inject a strong amount of personality. Now I'm focusing on traditional fonts too, which can be used in texts, and continue to transmit a strong sense of my own style at the same time.

What are your plans future plans for Typelab?

I aspire for **Typelab** to evolve through other mediums such as events, talks and other things. To continue to highlight young designers, building a valuable community and helping them connect for future collaborations.

@typelab.fr
www.typelab.fr

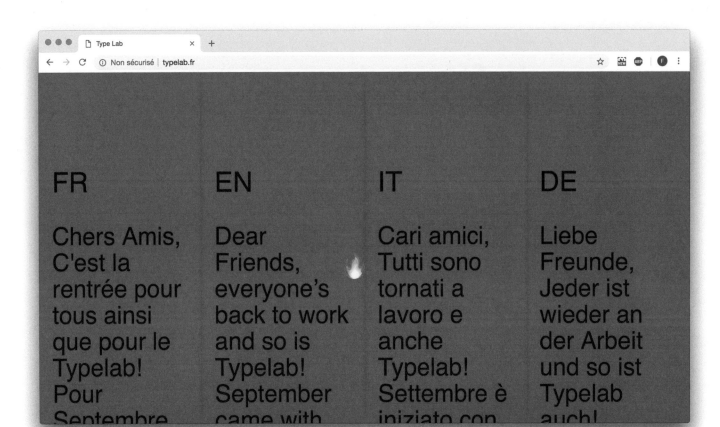

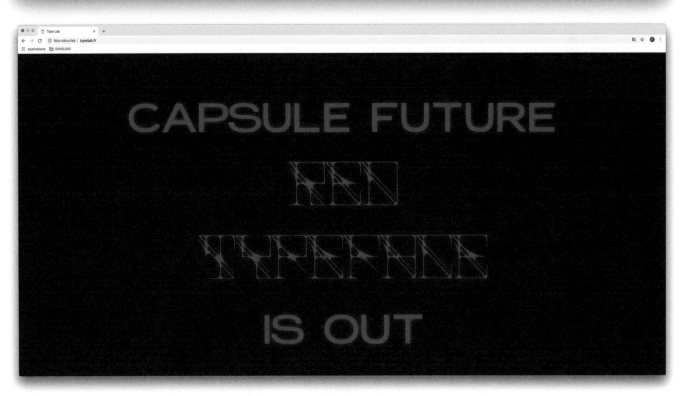

Typeface
Capsule Future
(2018)

67

a

Sages
typeface
Sages
typeface
Sages
typeface

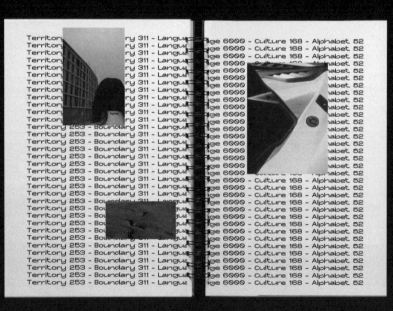

Territory 253 – Boundary 311 – Language 6000 – Culture 168 – Alphabet 52
Territory 253 – Boundary 311 – Language 6000 – Culture 168 – Alphabet 52
Territory 253 – Boundary 311 – Language 6000 – Culture 168 – Alphabet 52
Territory 253 – Boundary 311 – Language 6000 – Culture 168 – Alphabet 52
Territory 253 – Boundary 311 – Language 6000 – Culture 168 – Alphabet 52
Territory 253 – Boundary 311 – Language 6000 – Culture 168 – Alphabet 52
Territory 253 – Boundary 311 – Language 6000 – Culture 168 – Alphabet 52
Territory 253 – Boundary 311 – Language 6000 – Culture 168 – Alphabet 52
Territory 253 – Boundary 311 – Language 6000 – Culture 168 – Alphabet 52
Territory 253 – Boundary 311 – Language 6000 – Culture 168 – Alphabet 52
Territory 253 – Boundary 311 – Language 6000 – Culture 168 – Alphabet 52
Territory 253 – Boundary 311 – Language 6000 – Culture 168 – Alphabet 52
Territory 253 – Boundary 311 – Language 6000 – Culture 168 – Alphabet 52
Territory 253 – Boundary 311 – Language 6000 – Culture 168 – Alphabet 52
Territory 253 – Boundary 311 – Language 6000 – Culture 168 – Alphabet 52
Territory 253 – Boundary 311 – Language 6000 – Culture 168 – Alphabet 52
Territory 253 – Boundary 311 – Language 6000 – Culture 168 – Alphabet 52
Territory 253 – Boundary 311 – Language 6000 – Culture 168 – Alphabet 52
Territory 253 – Boundary 311 – Language 6000 – Culture 168 – Alphabet 52
Territory 253 – Boundary 311 – Language 6000 – Culture 168 – Alphabet 52
Territory 253 – Boundary 311 – Language 6000 – Culture 168 – Alphabet 52
Territory 253 – Boundary 311 – Language 6000 – Culture 168 – Alphabet 52

Specimen
Sages 01
Typeface

Like a desert
in the rain
When the sun
of the day
went down
The flavor is
so strong
I've missed it
so long now

Sages 01
Typeface

Sahar Afshar is a type designer and researcher from Iran. Her interest in typography during her years as a student at the University of Tehran led her to the University of Reading in the UK from which she holds an MA in Typography & Graphic Communication. Since graduation, Sahar has been working on the design, consultation and quality assurance of Arabic typefaces, as well as researching the printing of Arabic scripts.

Alphabettes.org Header
(2018)

Currently based in the UK, Sahar is a doctoral candidate at **Birmingham City University**, where she also works as a research assistant to the **Centre for Printing History and Culture**. Contributing to the well known all-female digital type discussion platform **Alphabettes.org**, Sahar submitted her floral Kufi and Thuluth calligraphic style type designs and was featured as one of the many winning typographic headers on the site.

@sahafshar
PHD Candidate

SAHAR AFSHAR

010

Founder of Koutour Type Foundry, Sibylle Hagmann is an established type designer within her field. Developing an innovative collection of fonts including Cholla, Kopius, Elido and Odile, Sibylle is also a professor at the University of Houston's School of Art.

Typeface
Elido Italic (2010)

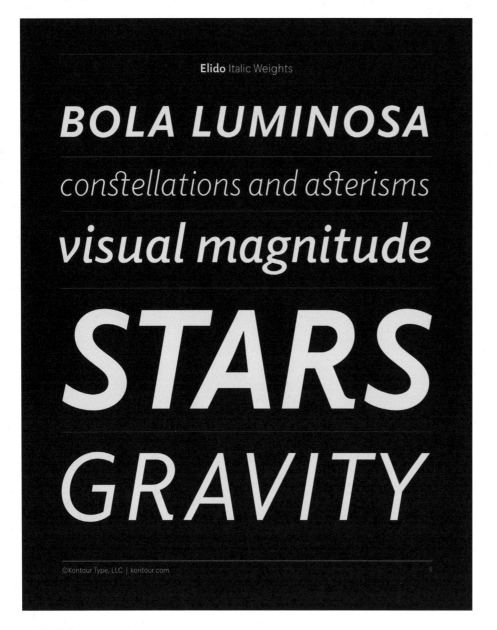

@sibyllehagmann
www.kontour.com

Published in 2010 **Elido** (Odile in reverse) is the sans counterpart to **Odile**, a serif type. Combined, they form a sans and serif superfamily with a wide range of variations for editorial and display use. **Elido** has 16 impressive weights, following **Odile's** proportions and matching the weight distribution and typographic colour of its serif twin. **Odile's** conceptual approach is echoed in the structure and anatomy of the Elido family. For example, the arched stroke low off the stem reveals a script characteristic most pronounced in the **Elido** Upright Italic. This particular interpretation is gradually diminished in the Italic and becomes even less emphasised in the Regular style.

A second typeface released and published in 2016 is the **Kopius** family, a contemporary serif type that features friendly characteristics with round, open counters conveying a relaxed ambiance. The robustness of the characters supports a wide variety of applications including editorial and display use. Defining elements of the face include the multitude of weights to satisfy any fanciful appetite for a colourful typographic palette. With packaging solutions in mind, the family includes sets of expandable and combinable box heading material for a boundless range of adjusted composites as well as pertinent labels, weight-adjusted arrows and word logos to complete the **Kopius** family.

Kopius Light
Kopius Light italic
Kopius Book
Kopius Book Italic
Kopius Regular
Kopius Regular Italic
Kopius Semibold
Kopius Semibold Italic
Kopius Bold
Kopius Bold Italic
Kopius Extrabold
Kopius Extrabold
Kopius Bold
Kopius Bold

Elido Light
Elido Light Italic
Elido Book
Elido Book Italic
Elido Regular
Elido Italic
Elido Semibold Italic
Elido Semibold
Elido Bold Italic
Elido Bold
Elido Black Italic
Elido Black

À Á Â Ã Ä Å Æ
Ç È É Ê Ë

Diacritics Uppercase / 48pt

! @ $ % * : ™ ° .

Punctuation / 48pt

a b c d e f g h i j k l m
n o p q r s t u v w x y z

Lowercase Book Italic / 48pt

ì í î ï è é ê ë ü ù ú û þ ÿ

Initials / 36pt

Box Headings / 36pt

ÁĂĂĂÀĀĄÅ
Å Ã Æ Æ

Diacritics Uppercase / 48pt

! @ $ % * : ™ ° ·

Punctuation /48pt

*abcdefghijklm
nopqrstuvwxyz*

Lowercase Book Italic / 48pt

ìíîïèéêëüùúûþÿ

Initials / 36pt

Ornaments / 36pt

THE ALPHABETTES HEADERS

In the late summer of 2015, **Alphabettes** started as a lengthy group email thread and has since evolved into an international network that supports and promotes women in type and the lettering arts. In the very early days, we imagined a place on the web to publish our own thoughts and writing. So we did what any self-respecting, overcommitted people do: we started a new side project. Within two weeks of registering **Alphabettes.org** in late August 2015 and through many late night, trans-Atlantic sessions of reckless intermediate Wordpress theme-editing, the scrappy and minimal site was live but needed one thing: a way to display our name — **Alphabettes**.

Rather than design a specific logotype or header, we decided to showcase the typefaces and lettering designed by the network of members and beyond to set the masthead of our fledgling site. Nearly every two weeks since then, over 80 headers have been featured in a range of scripts and styles. In addition to the rotating header, we also update, albeit much less frequently, the typefaces used on the blog. This provides a great opportunity to show off the work of type designers in the network and breaks the convention of maintaining a consistent typographic voice steadily over time.

We'd like to think that what makes the blog work is the general lack of hierarchy, internal structure, or editorial control. Leaving our egos at the door and making decisions via lazy consensus, we set out to create something that is spontaneous and topical, and leveraged the network's superpowers. Nearly four years later, the sites boasts over 260 published posts written by more than 50 contributors from around the world. From in-depth type design process reflections and showcases of historical artefacts to commentary on contemporary practices, the site has become an active voice — made up of many voices — in the type world. Like the network itself, the online archive of past headers illustrates

@alphabettes_org
www.alphabettes.org

This poster developed out of a request for a piece to be included in an exhibition at the 2018 conference, Tipografía México: The Future is Female. Displaying all of the headers (from 2015–2018) in this format reflects the composition of the group itself: linguistically diverse, stylistically broad, and slightly chaotic.

the diversity of perspectives and approaches of our contributors. For example, how does one translate the word "Alphabettes" into Arabic, Hebrew, or Gujarati? Sahar Afshar, Liron Lavi Turkenich, and Zenab Bastawala all discussed this in a post on the subject back in 2017. For Afshar, she chose to use a Persian transliteration for her Arabic header.

"This was fairly straightforward, except for two single letters, the 'S' and the 'T'. In Persian phonology, the /s/ phoneme can be represented with three letters (ث – ص – س) and the /t/ phoneme can be represented through two letters (ت – ط). I made the choice to stick to the most widely used form of each of these letters in different languages that use the Arabic script, namely the 'Sīn '(س) and the 'Tā' (ت). So for instance I could have used the 'Thā' (ث) for /s/, but this letter often corresponds to /th/ in the Arabic language, so I avoided it. As Persian is a gender-neutral language, my header is just a transliterated version of the English; however, I know this can be a point that needs deliberation for some languages."
— Sahar Afshar

For Lavi Turkenich, her header had the added challenge of considering grammatical genders in Hebrew.

"The word Alphabettes has to be female, so it would be ending on either 'h' (ה)in singular or 't' (ת) in plural. So if Alphabettes were a group of women, they would be "Alphabetot". Since there is no Hebrew word as such, but the ending is very Hebrewish, it looked odd. Luisa [Baeta] solved the problem when suggesting I should transliterate by thinking how I describe Alphabettes to my friends in Israel. I say Alphabettes just as it sounds! So now the ending is "ס", combining Hebrew letters and a Latin word."
— Liron Lavi Turkenich

In Bastawala's case, she chose to use the direct translation, "Varnamalao" (the proper translation of "alphabets" in Gujarati), "because of its sound and rhythm of the characters."

"It was fascinating when I was designing the header as per my style of character stacking, વર્ણમાળાઓ had very strong and box case title appearance which would be more visible as an identity. And the choice I made for the Gujarati characters were according to their open counters, vertical heights with less disturbing marks and flexibility of each other, so overall it happened to be a good combination of the characters."
— Zenab Bastawala

While the majority of headers feature published or in-progress typefaces, many showcase custom lettering or calligraphy. Headers have been carved, cut, painted, photographed, stamped, and embroidered. In most cases, the header is black on a white background, but several headers have incorporated colour, illustration and even emojis.

In some ways, **Alphabettes** is a feminist response to the traditional hierarchies of many design organisations and perhaps the ever-changing header helps reinforce our constantly evolving and collaborative approach to the initiative. We're not sure what the next three years will bring to the blog, but we are always open to new header submissions, no matter how you write, draw, or say it.

Words by Amy Papaelias.
Co-Founder of Alphabettes.org

ALPHABETTES
ALPHABETTES
Alphabettes
alphabettes
Alphabettes
alphabettes
ALPHABETTES
Alphabettes
Alphabettes
Alphabettes
Alphabettes
Alphabettes
Alphabettes
Alphabettes
Alphabettes
ALPHABETTES
Alphabettes
Alphabettes
Alphabettes
Alphabettes
alphabettes
Alphabettes
Alphabettes
Alphabettes
Alphabettes
Alphabettes
Alphabettes
Alphabettes, alphabettes
Alphabettes ♡
Alphabettes
AlphaBettes monoline
Alphabettes

The Headers*

01. Birdy, Veronika Burian
02. Tuscan typeface, Tânia Raposo
03. Custom lettering, Victoria Rushton
04. Magasin, Laura Meseguer
05. Chimera, Maria Doreuli
06. Blenny, Spike Spondike
07. Paroli, Elena Schneider
08. Beloved, Laura Worthington
09. In-progress typeface, Paula Mastrangelo
10. Bely, Roxane Gataud
11. Charma, Heidi Rand Sørensen
12. Eskapade, Alisa Nowak
13. Custom lettering, Lynne Yun
14. Custom lettering, Jen Mussar
15. Rakkas, Zeynep Akay
16. Custom lettering, Isabel Urbina Peña
17. Custom lettering, Pooja Saxena

18. Sastre, Maria Ramos
19. Maku (in-progress), Kimya Gandhi
20. Harlemite, Elizabeth Carey Smith
21. Pistachio Bugmese, Thalia Echevarria
22. Custom lettering, Liä Symons
23. Langar, Alessia Mazzarella
24. Nordwest, Nina Stössinger
25. LiebeGerda, Ulrike Rausch
26. Royal, Roxandra Duru
27. Paulette Bold (in-progress), Alice Savoie
28. Custom Arabic lettering, Sahar Afshar
29. Custom lettering, Azucena León
30. Kannada, Erin McLaughlin
31. Embury Text, Victoria Rushton
32. Linocut lettering, Marisol Ortega
33. Custom lettering, Jessica McCarty
34. Malis, Barbara Bigosińska

35. In-progress typeface, Elena Schneider
36. Lisbeth, Louisa Fröhlich
37. Custom lettering, Marina Chaccur
38. Volina, Francesca Bolognini
39. Custom Bengali lettering, Pooja Saxena
40. Junior, Selina Bernet
41. Plex, Kamilah Carter
42. ASCII lettering, Bianca Berning
43. Makeda, Liron Lavi Turkenich
44. In-progress typeface, Zenab Bastawala
45. Pilot, Aleksandra Samulenkova
46. Kufic lettering, Sahar Afshar
47. Devanagari lettering, Namrata Goyal
48. Capucine, Alice Savoie
49. Razeen Sans, Nadia Badran
50. Marianne Brandt Alphabet, Stéphane Dupont
51. Gautreaux, Victoria Rushton

52. Hangul lettering, June Shin
53. Noto Armenian, Elena Papassissa
54. LaIola, Laura Meseguer
55. Bree Cyrillic, Veronika Burian
56. Bitter Pro (Sol Matas) Embroidered, Marisol Ortega
57. Alkes Thai, Kaja Slojewska
58. Excon Medium, Alisa Nowak
59. Kinetic, Maria Ramos
60. Trade Gothic Display, Lynne Yun
61. Devanagari Lettering, Tanya George
62. Bizzarrini v0.1, Diana Ovezea and Sabina Chipară
63. Boutros Aura, Soulaf Khalifeh
64. Lettering, Snehal Patil
65. In-progress typeface, Amélie Bonet
66. Messer Italic, Inga Plönnigs
67. Cut paper lettering, Kelly Thorn
68. In-progress Khmer typeface, Natalie Rauch

69. Custom lettering, Ruxandra Duru
70. In-progress Devanagari typeface, Kimya Gandhi
71. Happy World Emoji Day, Alphabettes
72. Mukta Mahee Gurmukhi, Shuchita Grover
73. Green Fairy, Maria Montes
74. Bridge, Mona Franz
75. Farsan, Pooja Saxena
76. Naej, Blondina Elms Pastel
77. Duet (in-progress), Hendrika Makilya
78. Xihti, Dafne Martinez
79. Rose Light, Roxane Gataud
80. Custom lettering, Erin Ellis
81. Custom lettering, Aoife Mooney

* almost all, plus stamp lettering by Sol Matas

The Typefaces

Boly Display by Roxane Gataud
Dover Serif Text by Robin Mientjes
Elena by Nicole Dotin
Elido by Sibylle Hagmann
Pilot Semi-Bold by Aleksandra Samulenkova

2015–2018
Alphabettes.org

Laura Meseguer is a freelance type designer. Her works include solutions for international and domestic clients but also self-initiated projects.
As a typographer and type designer, she has specialised in all sorts of projects including custom lettering, typeface designs for branding and also publishing design.

àáâãäå

èéêë ìíîï

òóôõö «

Typeface
Qandus Original

@laurameseguer
www.laurameseguer.com

الخزعبلات

Gezellig

ⵀⵙⴻⵣⴰⵔⵓⵓ

Alegría!

ⴰⵛⵙⵣⵣⵀ

الإنتخابيّة

ⵉⵛⵝⵅⵅⵝⵓ

نعم للإستقلالية

Buffaloes

à á â ã ä å æ

è é ê ë ì í î ï

ò ó ô õ ö ù ú û ü

abcdefghijk
lmnopqrstu
vwxyz

% * ?

Typeface
Qandus Original

Qandus is a multiscript typeface system which aims to explore a conceptual relationship between 3 different writing systems: Arabic, Latin and Tifinagh. It started off as an homage to the work of Al-Qandusi, a brilliant and expressive calligrapher, and expanded into being a study of the unique combinations of Arabic constructions in the Maghribi calligraphic style, and how to disseminate this feature of duality of forms into the other two scripts. This project was developed as part of the **Typographic Matchmaking in the Maghrib** project of the **Khatt Foundation**. Laura was part of a team of three designers: Kristyan Sarkis for the Arabic, Juan Luis Blanco for the Tifinagh, and Laura for the Latin. By the time it's fully designed the complete system will consist of an impressive 27 fonts with three unique constructions.

Natalie Rauch is a type designer from Berlin who graduated from the University of Reading, UK in 2014. Since then, Natalie has been working as a freelancer on various type projects with a particular interest in foreign script systems.

Typeface
FiraGO Hebrew (2016)

FiraGO is a multi-script open source project that is based on **Fira Sans**. In 2016, the geo data provider Here chose **Fira Sans** as their corporate typeface and needed a wider language support. Natalie happily helped **FiraGO** to grow into one of the most important open source type families by designing the Hebrew script extension (Roman and Italics). **FiraGO Hebrew** has the lightest Hebrew weights ever designed and additionally benefits from a full set of Hebrew cantillation marks.

@natalierauch
www.natalie-rauch.com

עטלף אבק נס דרך מזגן שהתפוצץ כי חם

FiraGO Two

עטלף אבק נס דרך מזגן שהתפוצץ כי חם

FiraGO Four Italic

עטלף אבק נס דרך מזגן שהתפוצץ כי חם

FiraGO Eight

עטלף אבק נס דרך מזגן שהתפוצץ כי חם

FiraGO Hair Italic

עטלף אבק נס דרך מזגן שהתפוצץ כי חם

FiraGO Thin

עטלף אבק נס דרך מזגן שהתפוצץ כי חם

FiraGO Ultralight Italic

עטלף אבק נס דרך מזגן שהתפוצץ כי חם

FiraGO Extralight

עטלף אבק נס דרך מזגן שהתפוצץ כי חם

FiraGO Light Italic

עטלף אבק נס דרך מזגן שהתפוצץ כי חם

FiraGO Book

עטלף אבק נס דרך מזגן שהתפוצץ כי חם

FiraGO Regular Italic

עטלף אבק נס דרך מזגן שהתפוצץ כי חם

FiraGO Medium

עטלף אבק נס דרך מזגן שהתפוצץ כי חם

FiraGO Semibold Italic

עטלף אבק נס דרך מזגן שהתפוצץ כי חם

FiraGO Bold

עטלף אבק נס דרך מזגן שהתפוצץ כי חם

FiraGO Extrabold Italic

עטלף אבק נס דרך מזגן שהתפוצץ כי חם

FiraGO Heavy

ទំពាំងបាយជួរ

They are absolute rascals, those cheeky monkeys

moonhead

ភ្ជុំពេញ

Purple Thunderclouds

ពួនកលាង

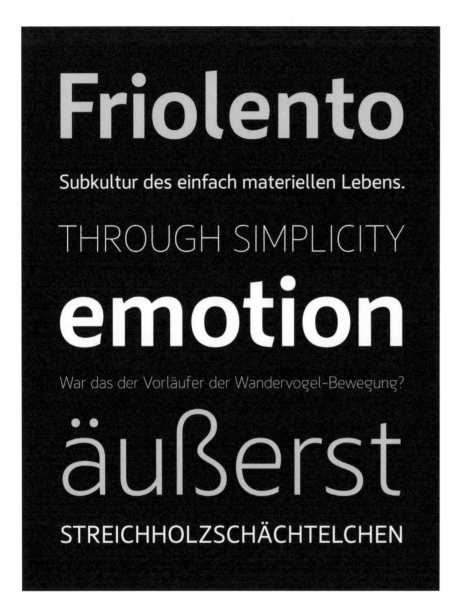

Typeface
Hedda (2017)

Natalie began the development of **Munny** in 2017. The concept and idea derived from a month spent in South East Asia whilst attending several type design workshops. This typeface family she is producing aims to make a contribution to producing a more diverse typographic landscape for local designers in Southeast Asia. Which is also why it, eventually, aims to unite all five different script systems in harmony: Khmer, Myanmar, Lao, Thai and Latin. Often other scripts systems follow the Latin whereas **Munny** puts Southeast Asian script systems at the forefront. Nevertheless, all of Natalie's typefaces constantly influence each other and are developed in parallel.

Working under the moniker Matra Type, India-based type designer Pooja Saxena has been creating her own letters, and designing with them since 2010. Pooja focuses on the languages and scripts used throughout India, harnessing her expertise in type design and typography to further projects with cultural and educational bents.

The Print
(2017)

Having taught introductory workshops in type design in several design institutions - **Srishti School of Design**, **Art and Technology**, **Pearl Academy**, and the **Indian Institute of Art & Design** - Pooja, along with being an active collaborator in **Delhi Typerventions**, single-handedly organised the event, an experimental lettering installation made from everyday materials to spell out meaningful messages in the city's public spaces in Bangalore between 2013–14. In early 2018, she launched **India Street Lettering**, an online map-based archive of street lettering from around the country showcasing the impressive and beautiful lettering artists work that paint the city of Delhi. Pooja's designs have been featured in Indian and international press, including **Scroll.in**, **Outlook Traveller**, **Make in India** magazine, **AIGA Eye on Design**, **TypeGeist** and **Adobe Create.**

@matratype
www.matratype.com

Coovum Art Festival
(2016)

Dr. Nadine Chahine is an award-winning Lebanese type designer. Nadine's work has been featured in the 5th edition of Megg's History of Graphic Design back in 2012 and was selected by Fast Company as one of its 100 Most Creative People in Business.

خط عناوين خاص بجريدة النهار

يا جبل ما يهزك ريح

صلب وقوي، منحوت بدقة

ء آ آ أ أ أ ؤ وَ إ إئ ئئ ا ا ب ببب ة بة ت تتت ت ثث ث ثثث ج ججج ج ححح ح خ
خخخ د د ذ ر ز سس ش ششش ص صصص ض ضضض
ط ططط ظ ظظظ ع ععع غ غغغ ف ففف ق ققق ك ككك ل للل م ممم ن
ننن ه ههه و و ى سى ي ييي أ ألا لا لآ لآ لأ لأ لإ لإ؟ !0123456789

الخط
الحظ
الخط
الحظ

Design is in the details.

Maria Doreuli is a Russian-born type designer who graduated with a MA degree in Type & Media from the University of Reading. Doreuli currently runs Contrast Type Foundry in Moscow, producing well crafted, beautiful font designs with her team of designers.

William Display for *LARGE* sizes & Interesting Headlines.

William Subhead for texts of *moderate* sizes.

William Text for efficient readability in medium and *small sizes*.

One of Maria's highly rated type designs include **William**, a contemporary interpretation of **Caslon**. **William** is a well balanced international font in which English, Dutch and Russian influences came together to create one complete, modern type family. **Caslon's** work has a permanent place in the typographic history whilst **William** builds on his foundation and makes this new face relevant for a new generation of designers. The font is available in three optical sizes, a Text version with a large x-height for smaller text from 7 to 12pt, a Subhead version for use at 14 to 30 points, and Display version for text larger than 36 points. Just as **Caslon** cut many non-Latin types and ornaments, **William** focuses on his international typography and supports Cyrillic and Greek.

A second typeface is **Chimera**, an experiment in bringing dynamism and beauty into the traditional reversed contrast typefaces. Historically these typefaces were intentionally created to be ugly: their letter forms were designed as the opposite of the elegant classics, and their strangeness deliberately challenged expectations and

grabbed attention. Defying the rules once more, **Chimera** twists this quirky concept into an elegant and versatile type family. Influenced by calligraphy with a broad-nib tool held at a steep 45° angle, the quirkiness is suddenly transformed into friendliness.

Intended especially for display use, the typeface includes 3 high-contrast statement styles and 2 low-contrast companions. The low-contrast styles retain the same daring character, but are adjusted to perform well in smaller sizes. All the styles in the family are based on the same concept and share certain characteristics, but each font is drawn completely from scratch bringing its uniqueness to the mix for each design.

@doreuli
www.contrastfoundry.com

EXPERIMENTING WITH TRADITIONAL RESTRICTIONS

Reversed Queen

EXTRAORDINARY AND IMPRESSIVE LOOK

EXPERIMENT WITH THE REVERSED BROAD-NIB MODEL

IMPLAUSIBLE MONSTER

THE MAIN DESIGN FEATURES OF THE TYPEFACE
ARE VERY BIG X-HEIGHT AND NARROW PROPORTIONS

Typeface
Chimera (2018)

The New Normal

Benjamin H.Bratton

Typeface: William Display
(2008-2018)

•Mad•

•Insane•

•Nuts•

•Absurd•

•Wild•

012₴
₽34
567€
¥89

1. "What's New in Swift". Apple Developer (Video). June 14, 2016. At 2:40. Retrieved June 16, 2016.

2. Juli Clover (April 24, 2018). "Apple Releases macOS High Sierra 10.13.4 Security Update". MacRumors.

3. "macOS High Sierra 10.13.4 (17E202)—Releases". Apple Developer. Apple Inc. April 24, 2018.

4. Juli Clover (April 17, 2018). "Apple Seeds Second Beta of macOS High Sierra 10.13.5 to Developers". MacRumors. Retrieved April 18, 2018.

5. "macOS High Sierra 10.13.5 beta (17B45c)—Releases—Apple Developer". developer.apple.com. April 17, 2018. Retrieved April 18, 2018.

6. "macOS – How to Upgrade – Apple". Apple. Retrieved September 28, 2016.

7. Apple Events—WWDC Keynote June 2016. Event occurs at 36:28.

8. "Desktop Operating System Market Share". Net Applications.

9. "Top 8 Operating Systems from Sept 2011 to Aug 2015".

10. Ha, Anthony (June 10, 2013). "Apple Has A New, California-Based Naming Scheme For OS X, Starting With OS X Mavericks". TechCrunch. Retrieved June 10, 2013. macOS Server — Mac App Store.

11. "Mac OS X Version 10.5 on Intel-based Macintosh computers". The Open Group. Retrieved December 4, 2014.

12. "Mac OS X Version 10.6 on Intel-based Macintosh computers". The Open Group. Retrieved December 4, 2014.

13. "Apple technology brief on UNIX" (PDF). Apple. Retrieved November 5, 2008.

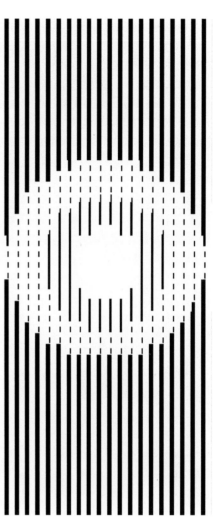

CoFo Sans
(2016-2018)

One final example of Maria's type work with the help of Liza Rasskazova and Irina Smirnova, **CoFo Sans** is a clean sans-serif with a soul. This is not just another neutral sans. Arguably, one of the most challenging things when creating a font is to portray simplicity in its construction. Yet many sans-serifs exist that claim to be completely neutral and perfectly universal. **CoFo Sans** is based on the idea of harmony between rationality and emotion, between Latin and Cyrillic. It's the designers' perception of a perfect balance between simplicity and personality. It's not purely geometric, or even based on a specific model. **CoFo Sans** is subtle, an interesting mix of ideas, creating a solid base for a workhorse sans without stripping away its character. The strong squareness of the letter forms and a trace of industrial functionality have been mixed in the designer's intuition, to make **CoFo Sans** unique. Simplicity doesn't need dozens of weights, widths and styles, so **CoFo Sans** comes in 4 individual and carefully drawn weights: Regular, Medium, Bold and Black.

New York-based Senior Designer TienMin Liao has established herself as a well-known type guru, having designed bespoke typefaces for Fortune 100 companies and worked on various logotype projects for global organisations, including CVS, Birchbox, Wyndham, Verizon, Resideo, Hungryroot, USP and many more. Earlier last year she was named one of the Ascenders 2018 by the Type Directors Club, a prestigious award and title.

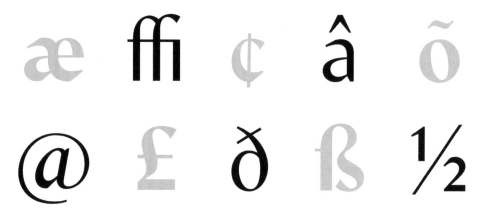

Typeface
Mins Sans

TienMin studied typeface design at **The Cooper Union** and now works with **Siegel+Gale**, **Prophet**, **Monotype**, the **Type Directors Club** and many more constructing her type creations from Long Island, New York. Some of her projects include the Bilingual Lettering project which is a series of Latin - Kanji pairing studies for use in bilingual lettering and logotypes and **Min Sans**. A high contrast sans serif type family designed to be used in art & fashion publications. The sharp notch and clean contour design exudes a strong personality and contemporary look

@tienmin_liao
typeji.com

Min Sans is **a high contrast sans serif type family** designed to be used in art and fashion publications.

Ligature

fl → fl

fi → fi

ff → ff

taffies
muffins
figures
selfies
surfboat
flavor
selfheals
office
waffle

Numerals

£193

47%

8½

2.69/ea
4 for 8.19
April 26
b.1914
2019-3-21
#280
Oct. 17
1967-1998
$29.49

Cufflinks can be manufactured from a variety of different materials. The first cufflinks appeared in the 1600s.

Einstein, Albert (1954), *Ideas and Opinions*, New York: Random House, ISBN 0-517-00393-7

Lilly Marques is London-based, freelance experiential product designer, tech and type enthusiast. Lilly has a systematic approach to design and above all is drawn to the methodical nature of designing letterforms. Creating systems which fit the purpose of the product allows the design to be well informed and impactful, therefore suiting the purpose at hand.

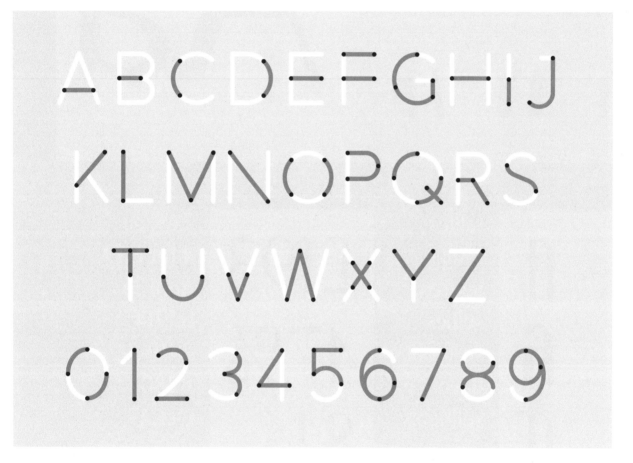

Custom Typeface
Inovation Centre
(2018)

@_lillymarques
www.lillymarques.com

A SPACE FOR URBAN INNOVATORS TO WORK TOGETHER AND CREATE CITIES OF THE FUTURE

Custom Typeface
Inovation Centre
(2018)

The Urban Innovation Centre, home to **Future Cities Catapult**, is a space for innovators and creators. The project identity focuses on the idea of connecting people and cities and works in parallel to **Future Cities** branding. The design which was created by Lilly is a flexible typographic system, custom type, crafted for this project. The system is formed of three connected layers — base, line and point. The combination integrates the brand and allows it to adjust its tone of voice depending on its communications as an organisation.

LILLY MARQUES

019

AaBbCcDdEeFfGg
HhIiJjKkLlMmNn
OoPpQqRrSsTtUu
VvWwXxYyZz

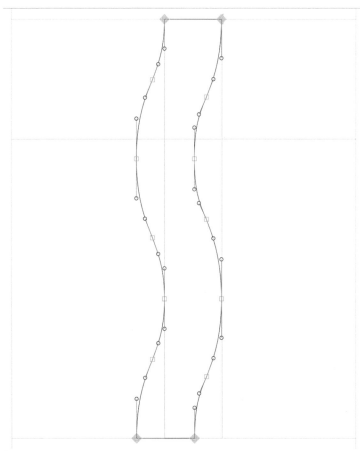

Custom Type Construction
Typeface: Inflo (2018)

A second typeface of Lilly's is for **Inflo**, a new publishing platform showcasing a fresh way for people to discover and create stories. The identity is inspired by the way users navigate through the sea of content. The design is an interchangeable typographic custom type, crafted for this project. It allows certain letters to be "in the flow", abstractly showing how stories are formed.

Charlotte Rohde is a Germany-based
Graphic Designer with a huge passion
for typography, typeface design
and type in pretty much all its forms.
Charlotte is also fascinated by type
related text topics which expands
beyond the design itself, exploring
the way in which type design can be
used for understanding and shaping
discourses beyond their literal content.

Typeface
Calyces (2018)

@charlotte__rohde
www.charlotterohde.de

sepals are called
the »calyx«
(plural calyces),[7]
the outermost
whorl of parts that

Calyces is one of Rohde's many great typefaces designed to be read like opera – sharp, romantic and elegant with a hint of pathos. The name **Calyces** derives from the floral forms of the letter typically used in feminist projects and causes. "I believe that design doesn't need a feminist concept to do feminist actions," says Rohde.

Another font created by Charlotte is **Marguerite Grotesk**, a classic sans serif typeface named after Marguerite Gautier, the main character of the novel **'La Dame aux Camélias'** by Alexandre Dumas jr., published in 1848. Constructed in four weights, this project is an observation on gender roles in that novel, picking up the characteristics of the female lead character and putting it into form. The protagonist Marguerite is objectified in her role as a courtesan throughout the novel, however is also a very strong and decisive woman. The typeface Rohde created resembles that with very round, pleasing, but room-taking and stable forms resulting in a dramatic font that has a romantic air as words spread across the page.

ABCDEFGHIJKLMN
OPQRSTUVWXYZ
abcdefghijklmn
opqrstuvwxyz
1234567890/1234567890
!?$€£§↖©↘®

KᚴK
ƐEƐ

Typeface
Calyces (2018)

Bezirksamt Neukölln
Karl-Marx-Str. 83
12043 Berlin
Tel.: 4930 90239 0
Behörden-Hotline: 115

9 Rue d'Antin
75002 Paris

Typeface
Marguerite Grotesk

AÁÂÄÀÅÃÆBCČÇDÐEÉÊËÈFGHIÍÎÏJKLM
NÑOÓÔÖÒØÕŒPÞQRRSŞŠTUÚÛÜÙWŴ
ŴẄẀXYÝŶŸỲZaáâäàåãæaàáâãäåbcčç
dðeéêëèfghiıíîïïjjklmnñoóôöòøõœpþqrsş
šßtuúûüùvwẃŵẅẁxyýŷÿỳz
ﬀ ﬅ ﭅ ﭅ ﱔ ﬃ
0123456789
*\·•:,...!¡#.?¿'";//_{}[]()-—–
»«‹›„""''‚¢$€££¥+−×÷=>< %@&§©®®™°|¦†‡

Typeface
Marguerite(2018)

AÁÂÄÀÅÃÆBCČÇDÐEÉÊËÈFGHIÍÎÏJKL
MNÑOÓÔÖÒØÕ   PÞQRRSŞŠTUÚÛÜÙV
WẂŴẄẀXYÝŶŸỲZaáâäàåã   aàáâã
äåbcčçdðeéêëèfghiıíîï̈ìjjklmnñoóôöò
øõ   p   qrsşšßtuúûüùwẃŵẅẁxyýŷÿỳz
ﬀ ﬅ ﭅ ﭅ ﬃ ﭅
0123456789
*\·•:,...!¡#.?¿'";//_{}[]()-—–
»«‹›„""''‚¢$€£   ¥+−×÷=>< %@&§©®®™°|¦†‡

AÁÂÄÀÅÃÆBCČÇDÐEÉÊËÈFGHIÍÎÏJKL
MNÑOÓÔÖÒØÕŒPÞQRRSŠŞTUÚÛÜÙ
VWŴŴŴXYÝŶŸŶZaáâäàåãæaàáâã
äåbcčçdðeéêëèfghiıíîïìjjklmnñoóôöòø
õœpþqrsšşßtuúûüùvwẃŵẅẁxyýŷÿỳz
ff ft tt tf fft ttf
0123456789
*\•:,...!¡#.?¿"";//_{}[]()-—-
»«‹›„""'",¢$€££¥+−×÷=><%@&§©®®™°¦¦†

AÁÂÄÀÅÃÆBCČÇDÐEÉÊËÈFGHIÍÎÏJK
LMNÑOÓÔÖÒØÕŒPÞQRRSŠŞTUÚÛÜ
ÙVWŴŴŴŴXYÝŶŸŶZaáâäàåãæaà
áâãäåbcčçdðeéêëèfghiıíîïìjjklmnñoóô
öòøõœpþqrsşşšßtuúûüùvwẃŵẅẁx
yýŷÿỳz ff ft tt tf fft ttf
0123456789
*\•:,...!¡#.?¿"";//_{}[]()-—-
»«‹›„""'",¢$€££¥+−×÷=><%@&§©®®™°¦¦†

Descended from a grandfather who was part of the team of sign painters who worked on the infamous ship Titanic, Rachel Joy Price is a naturally talented lettering artist based in London. Rachel's work is versatile, spanning a variety of media from traditional sign paintings to crafting scripts and logo type for brands and packaging, 3D type within a VR world, murals, videos and books.

Book Cover Design
(2018)

@racheljoylettering
www.racheljoyprice.com

Custom Letters
(2017)

RACHEL JOY PRICE

021

Sign Commissions
(2015)

In what started as a experimental personal project, Rachel took photographs throughout her travels, capturing letters of a dry cleaner's signs, in Paris, or from a chunky bit of type from a builder's sign, an old poster in a museum, or more recently a trip to Kenya. Taking inspiration from these shapes and signs, she then adapts them, pulling the proportions around, transforming it into 3D. She then continues to spend around three hours pushing colours around.

Thanks to the growing popularity Rachel has gained on Instagram, she now sells them as giclee prints to her community of letter-loving customers. Sign commissions also make up a large part of Rachel's workspace. Although having worked with a lot of different branding and advertising agencies collaborating with some really great brands, Rachel is keen to keep the balance between the amount of digital work and traditional craft of sign painting she does: ending a day with hands covered in paint splatters is always a good one. Rachel learnt her skills from a sign course with Nick Garret back in 2016 which equipped her with the skills needed to produce her work. After completing a custom sign for a family member, her work snowballed and has now turned into a real constant stream of commissions, mainly coming in through Instagram. To date, Rachel has painted over 150 signs.

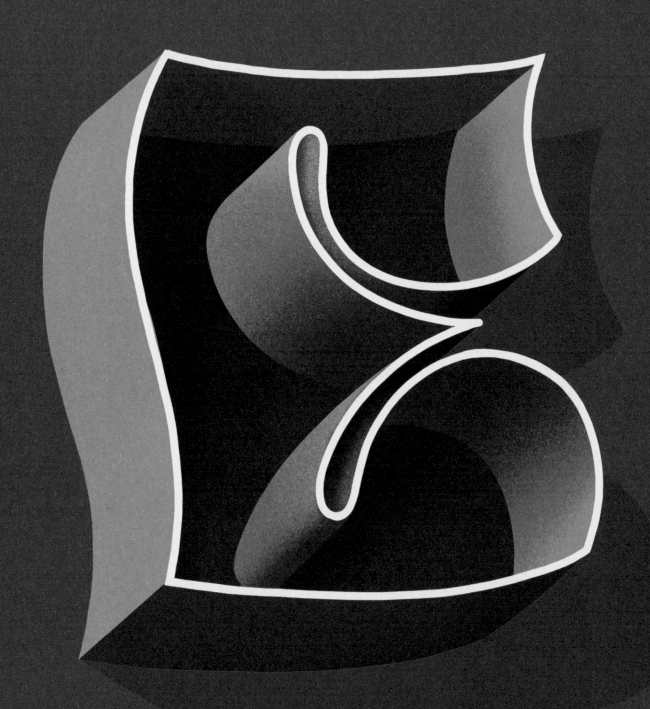

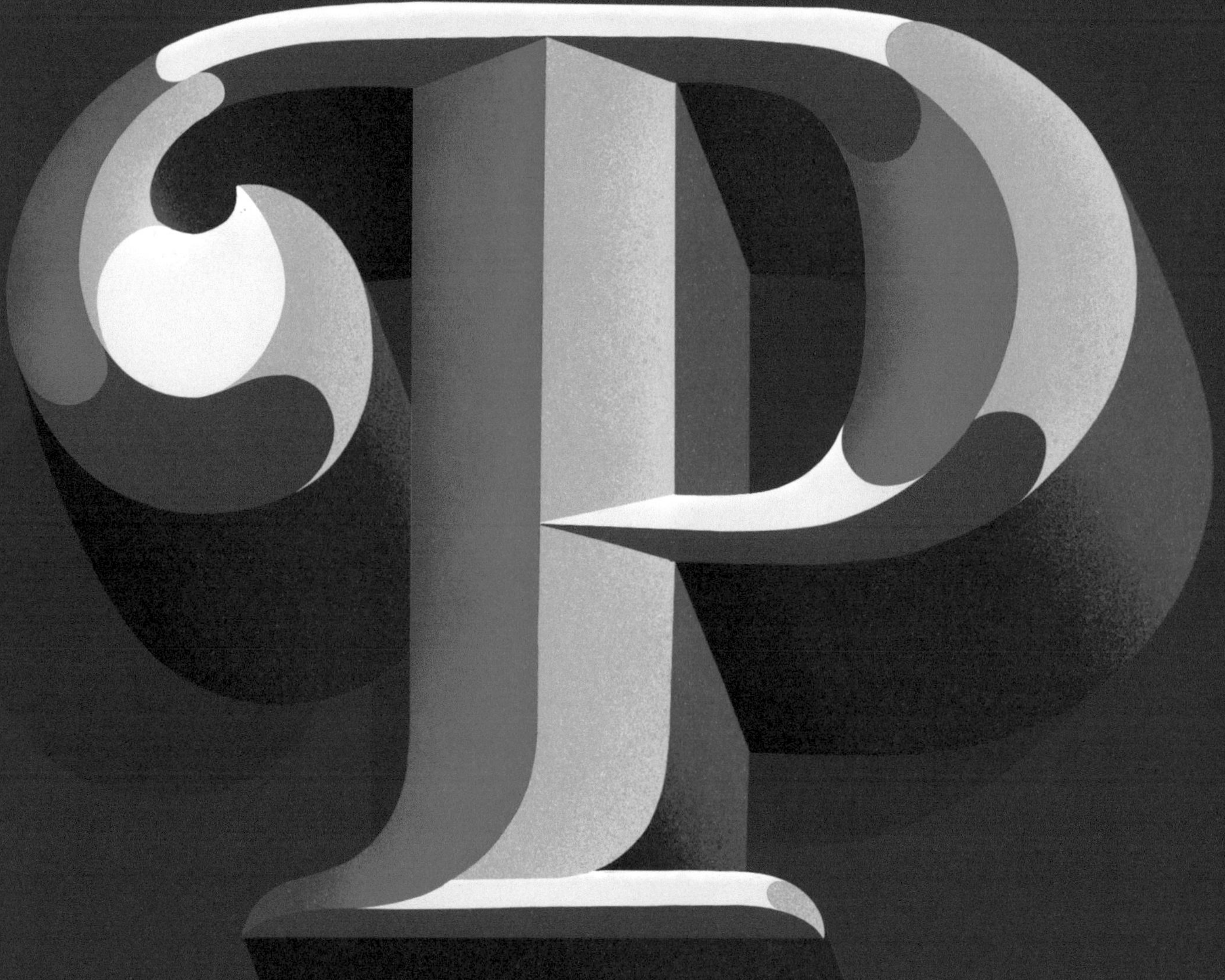
P

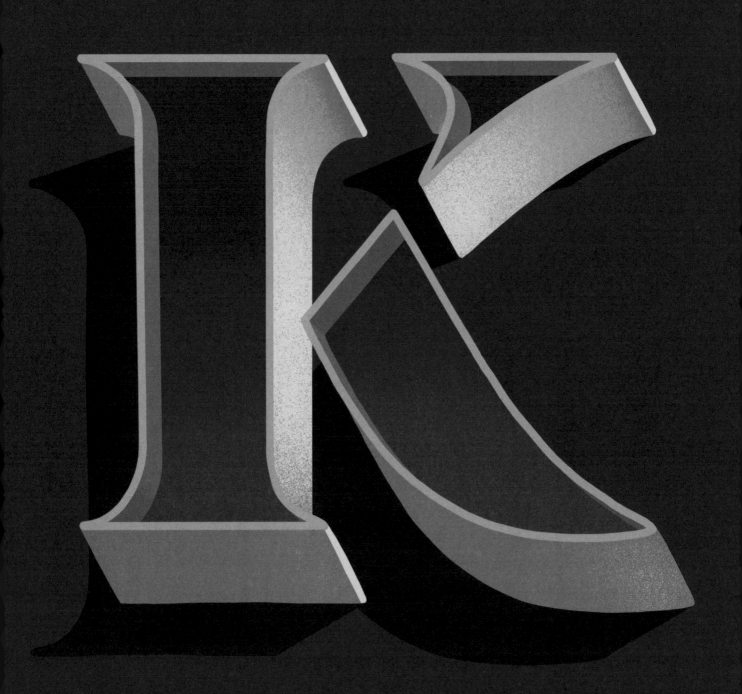

Ana Duje is an Argentinian graphic designer and illustrator currently living and working between two ends of the globe, Barcelona and Hong Kong. Throughout her work Ana follows one motto - less is certainly more. Using vibrant colour palettes and simple textures, she creates anthropomorphic figures from geometric shapes producing her own playful imitation of reality.

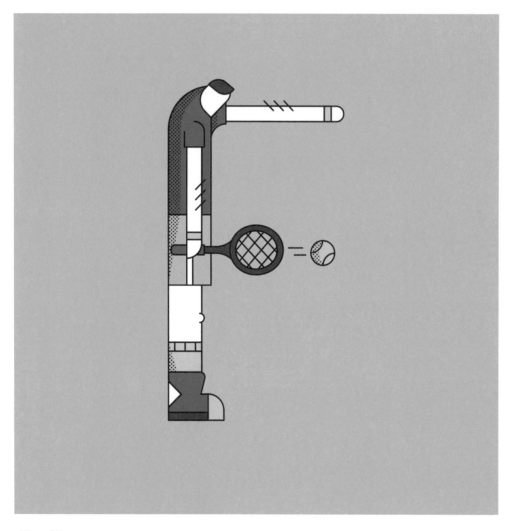

36 Days of Type
(2018)

@anaduje.design
www.anaduje.com

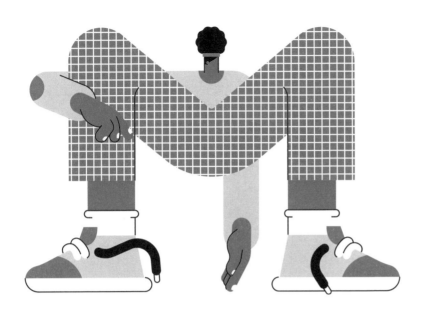

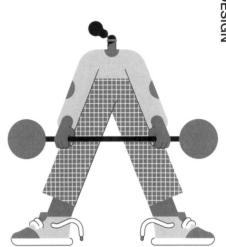

36 Days of Type
(2019)

Submitted as part of the **36 Days of Type** editions in 2018 and 2019, Ana projected her illustrative style onto her letter forms incorporating playful street/skater style characters. Her contribution showcases just one of the many contrasting contexts in which type is used, moving away from the typical editorial use where function and readability is most significant. What will always be quite a fascinating topic, is to see how alphabetic letter forms are used as a common base for designers who then project their creative styles and perspectives onto each letter creating a personal and individual language aesthetic.

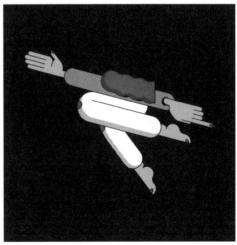

Joana Correia is the founder of Nova Type, a Porto-based independent foundry that creates font families and cultivates upcoming designers as they develop their work into finished fonts. Having studied architecture and graphic design and continuing on to acquire an MA in Typeface Design from University of Reading in 2011, one of Joanna's many achievements include winning a Granshan award for the Artigo font family.

The first of Nova's many typefaces is **Artigo Display**, the odd sister of the **Artigo** text typeface. Artigo Display is a contemporary interpretation of handwriting shapes in a display version of the italic. It is more expressive and it has its own personality with only a single weight (for now) but lighter weights are in progress. **Artigo Display** won a prestigious **Certificate of Typographic Excellence** from the **Type Directors Typeface Competition** in January 2018.

Next follows the regular counterpart **Artigo**, an old style inspired typeface system for text. **Artigo** was inspired by the handwriting aspect of the first roman types but it intends to be a contemporary interpretation. Its abilities are in small texts with a pinch of personality. The italics capture a lot of its dynamics, feeling even more expressive on the display version. This project began at the **University of Reading** while attending the **MA Typeface Design** in 2011. The project naturally grew and now supports Greek and Cyrillic. The Greek counterpart also won second prize in the Granshan Awards in 2011.

One final example of Nova's font productions is **Laca**, a semi-sans serif inspired by retro Portuguese soap packaging. **'Laca'** is the Portuguese word for hairspray and the initial starting point was to design a typeface that would bring a familiar feeling of closeness and warmth but giving it a modern look, ensuring it works well on modern platforms. **Laca** is perfect for branding and all types of communications. Additional features include an upright italic version available through the stylistic set that brings even more friendliness to the font. The result is a versatile typeface that has many OpenType features that bring stylistic alternatives to the designer.

@novatypefoundry
www.novatypefoundry.com

Typeface
Artigo Black
(2011)

The quick *brown fox* jumps over a *lazy dog.*

nova

Typeface
Artigo (2011)

Laca Extralight

Laca Light

Laca Book

Laca Regular

Laca Medium

Laca Semibold

Laca Bold

Laca Black

nova

Typeface
Laca (2018)

abcdefghij

klmnopqr

stuvwxyz

nova

Supertramp
Razzmatazz
Equivoques
Minimalism

Inga is an independent type designer based in Berlin. Inga divides her time between commissions for international clients and self initiated projects. Her work is inspired by history, necessity and the vernacular.

Typeface
Magnet

Magnet is a modern grotesque typeface with opportunistic contrast. Intended for display and editorial use such as posters, storefronts and magazines, it exhibits very condensed letter shapes and various unconventional design solutions. Deep notches, and the incisive stroke contrast in 'M' and 'W' make the typeface stand out without coming across as too conspicuous. **Magnet** includes an upright, slanted and backslanted style and there's also a matching text typeface with weights varying from Thin to Black. These two styles take the distinctive design ideas developed for **Magnet** Headline and turn them into something suitable for smaller sizes.

Messer on the other hand started out as a revival of Weiss Antiqua which was originally designed by Emil Rudolf Weiß in 1928. Along with Weiss Antiqua's signature characters and the upsidedown 's' and 'S', **Messer** also features similar design characteristics in 'z', 'ß', '6' and '9'. Compared to the original, the overall shapes have sharper edges and the Italic has less curly stroke endings. There is also a condensed display style that features an increased contrast to enhance the face's typographic possibilities.

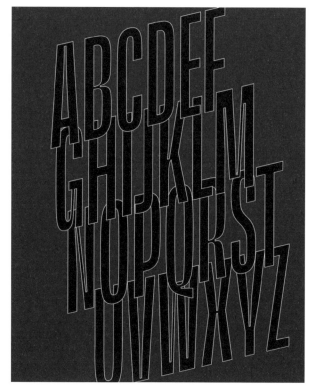

@ingaploennigs
www.ingaploennigs.com

130

M M
& &
G G

INGA PLÖNNIGS

024

ABCDEFG
HIJKLMN
OPQRST
UVWXYZ
abcdefghij
klmnopqr
stuvwxyz
0123456789

Typefaces
Left: Messer
Right: Magnet

Magnets don't need power.
Magnets don't need power.
Magnets don't need power.
Magnets don't need power.
Magnets don't need power.
Magnets don't need power.
Magnets don't need power.
Magnets don't need power.
Magnets don't need power.
Magnets don't need power.
Magnets don't need power.
Magnets don't need power.
Magnets don't need power.
Magnets don't need power.
Magnets don't need power.
Magnets don't need power.

Sandrine Nugue is an independent Type & Graphic Designer based in Paris, France. It was whilst studying for her postgraduate degree where she designed the Ganeau type family. She now divides her time between her graphic design and type design practice whilst also lecturing and teaching workshops in France and abroad.

Typeface
Infini (2018)

Typeface
Infini (2018)

Infini typeface was Sandrine's very first public commission by **The Centre National des Arts Plastiques** and **Orientation**, a stencil type family with the foundry **Commercial Type**. Both **Infini** and her next type design, **Orientation**, received the **Certificate of Excellence in Type Design** from the **Type Directors Club** of New York and in 2018, Sandrine was also awarded a prize as **Young Designer** by the city of Paris.

Infini is composed as a roman font with ligatures, pictograms and an italic. The face is bristly in display sizes, supple for text and the italic is a faithful partner for the roman, yet independent and the bold is oversized to overshadow its neighbours. The idea of the commission was to express to the general public what type design is and how type is constructed from its origins to our actual uses. Based on ancient gravestone writing, this is where the name **Infini** originated from: to talk about evolution without end.

Constructed as a stencil typeface, **Orientation** was a font commissioned by the graphic designer Thanh Phong Lê with the brief of creating a geometric typeface that could be fabricated as stencils for the way-finding system of a new student residence in Roubaix (France). The face was then expanded to a full family tree of three weights and matching italics released with **Commercial Type** last year.

orientation

light

direction

regular

location

bold

circulation

roman

situation

position

orientation

direction

italic

location

Zimbabwe Armenia
Danemark Sicilia
New Zealand España
Perú Switzerland
Liechtenstein Syria
Slovakia Madagascar
Uzbekistan Taïwan

Typeface
Orientation (2018)

Dr. Alice Savoie is an independent typeface designer and researcher. She studied typography in Paris, and in 2006 graduated from the MA Typeface Design at the University of Reading. Since then Alice has collaborated with international type foundries including Monotype, Process Type Foundry, Tiro Typeworks, Frere-Jones Type and OurType, specialising in the design of typefaces for editorial and branding purposes.

@alice_savoie
www.frenchtype.com

ier obstacle q

cette grande

ous ces différe

à les reconn

Typeface
Faune (2018)

f f f f f f f f

a a a a a a a a

u u u u u u u u

n n n n n n n n

e e e e e e e e

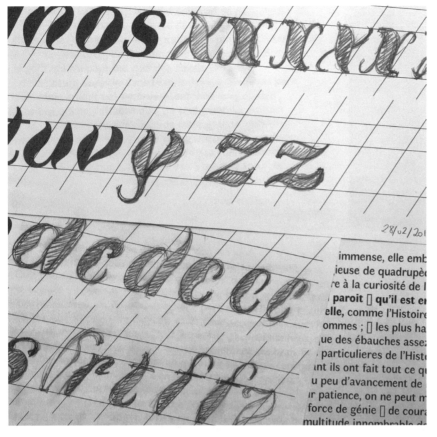

Typeface
Faune (2018)

Between 2008 and 2010 Alice joined **Monotype** as an in-house type
designer, working on custom projects for international clients and on
new typefaces for the **Monotype** library. In 2014 Alice was awarded a PhD
from the **University of Reading** for her research on typeface design and
production during the phototypesetting era. In 2018, she released **Faune**,
a commission by the **Centre National des Arts Plastiques**. The **Faune** type
family explores the plurality of the animal world and the diversity of its
morphologies. The face is based on two great reference works that were
both produced by the F**rench Imprimerie Nationale: Histoire naturelle by
Buffon** (1749–1788) and the **Description de l'Égypte**, commissioned by the
Emperor Napoleon 1st (1809–1830). Three categories of animals found in
these books (reptiles, birds and mammals) formed the basis for a diverse
typographic grammar. Thus, the sinewy viper inspired the design of the Thin
variant, while the stocky ram dictated the design of the Bold. The black
ibis was at the origin of the very particular design of the Italic. These three
founding members of the type family, with their very distinctive features,
were then rendered "genetically compatible" through an interpolation
process that resulted in three hybridisations, which proved to be perfectly
adapted to continuous reading at text sizes.

SLANTED PUBLISHERS

Julia Kahl studied Communication Design at the University of Applied Sciences in Darmstadt before she moved to Karlsruhe in 2007 to join the **Slanted** project. Here she was exposed to writing and editorial work, which gave her more satisfaction beyond being just a graphic designer. Back then, her main focus was to establish **Slanted** as a professional magazine and blog with a worldwide distribution and awareness. She built up a broad network of designers from all over the world that led to other design-related projects and publications in the fields of typography, graphic design, illustration and photography. In 2014 she went on to set up the publishing and media house **Slanted Publishers** together with Lars Harmsen. Slanted was born from a great passion for type and its growing industry and has made a name for itself across the globe. Its design is vibrant and inspiring — its philosophy open-minded, tolerant and curious.

Tell us how you came to set up Slanted? Was there a need for it?

When we started the **Slanted** blog (www.slanted.de) in 2004, it was meant to be a platform for exchange with friends from the cultural field about design and typography. It was a time where "blogs" had just started and it was interesting for us to write an article and tell our friends on the phone to have a look when it was online. More and more people who were involved in the platform were commenting and sharing the articles, so we got an incredible influx in a short time. In 2005 we felt the need to slow down the speed of the digital platform and to dig deeper into the field of typography and graphic design. Of course it was challenging and it always is to edit and publish a magazine, because in the beginning we did not know how to do it "right" and since then we've been improving the processes and our work to keep it running. When I started working for Slanted, most of the things I did were self-taught. I didn't know how to distribute a magazine when we had the first big print-run – I actually studied graphic design. I just called the important book stores and asked them whether they would be interested in having some of our magazines in stock. We had no subscriptions, advertising or a frequent publishing schedule. It was a huge amount of learning by doing and sometimes things worked out fine, sometimes they didn't. It was just 10 years after **Slanted** began that we were able to separate it from the design studio where it had its roots and set it up as an independent publishing house run by Lars Harmsen and me. Slanted was – and still is first and foremost – a passion-fueled project.

Seeing type on a day to day basis, what's the most interesting project you've seen recently?

A project that has had a great influence on many other projects - and probably even had a lasting influence on type design in terms of variable fonts in general - is Laurence Penney's Axis-Praxis (https://www.axis-praxis.org). It is a website for designers to try out variable fonts in a simple typesetting interface, and for font makers to test and show off their own variable fonts. Today, there are numerous examples of

www.slanted.de
www.volcano-type.de
www.yearbookoftype.com

Heldane

eface of the Month: Heldane

Type Foundry

the Neanderthal face, Heldane is a
d, a bastard, a fabrication. I vultured my
hrough history picking the bones from...

2019 ~ typography

All Jobs

total armageddon—a slanted reader on design

20+1. Ein Vergleich von ausgewählten serifenlosen Schriften der letzten zwanzig Jahre.

18,00 € Buy

Symbolwelt Bangladeschs

19,80 € Buy

Typotopografie, 7: Shanghai

14,80 € Buy

LOS ANGELES

30,00 € Buy

great variable fonts, and companies are beginning to dare to use variable custom fonts.

The font designers at Underware, who introduced Higher Order Interpolation for Variable Fonts in 2018, go one step further. In their case study, they explain the basic principles of more advanced interpolation that is no longer based on lines but on curves, without the complicated maths (www.underware.nl/case-studies/hoi).A current project of Hannah Witte is the variable Emojis. Created as a Variable Font, they give the users over thousands of options \to create an individual look with only one emoji (www.variableemojis.com/).

Your Yearbook of Type is one of our favourite publications - what's been the highlight of creating these publications?

The Yearbook of Type presents an independent selection of new typefaces created all over the world — from larger publishers to smaller, independent typographers and foundries. Although we are in touch with several hundred designers in every issue, we get to know new font designers each time — it's incredible to see what great typefaces there are all over the world, how different they are and how high the technical standard is nowadays.

Do you have another Yearbook of Type in the pipeline?

Yes, we do! The next issue will be published in the Autum of 2019. Starting this year, the book will be published annually and we've also planned some improvements for this issue: among other things we will lower the selling price, so that really every student can afford a book. After all the compendium is a source of inspiration and helps select the right typeface. In addition, there will also be more space for essays, tutorials and interviews where we will pick up on current topics and provide assistance.

Slanted Publishers
Yearbook of Type 3 (2018)

Finally, what is your current favourite typeface and why?

Since my studies I have followed and admired the work of Swiss Typefaces (www.swisstypefaces.com) and must admit that although I have a very great interest in all new publications, I often fall back on their writings. They have a very special style that suits my work very well. I particularly like the **Suisse Int'l** designed by Ian Party, our house font by **Slanted Publishers**, and of course **Sang Bleu**, which I discovered for the first time in 2009 on the magazine of the same name by Maxime Buechi. Among recently published writings I find Temeraire by Quentin Schmerber (www.type-together.com/temeraire-font) very exciting. Its obvious inconsistency in the cuts always brings surprises in all areas of its use.

Globalisation leads to bigger competition and more visibility globally so designers need to be very precise and have even more outstanding ideas in the future. There have always been lots of designers as well as good bakeries or restaurants – the best and most original will survive!

Erica Carras is a type designer based in Brooklyn. With a BFA from the Rhode Island School of Design and a certificate in type design from the Cooper Union Extended program of 2018, she has rich experience in both the production and designing of fonts for clients.

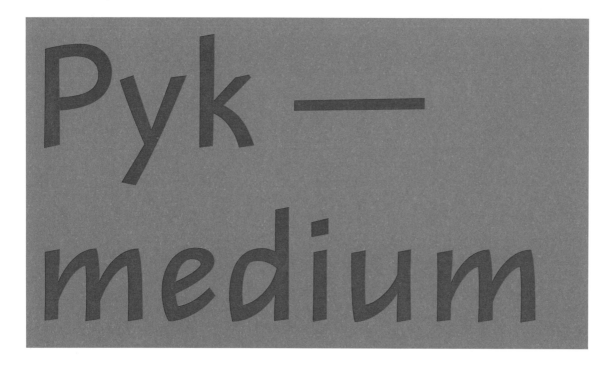

Inspired by Helmut Salden's brush lettering and punk rock posters, the process of taking a running hand (italic) system of calligraphy into an upright text face gave **Pyk** its unconventional letter shapes. In return, it gained a dramatic visual rhythm. **Pyk** will be available through **Future Fonts** later this year (2019).

@tiny_typo_
www.ericacarras.com

a b c d e f g h i j
k l m n o p q r s
t u v w x y z

← ↑ → ↓ ↖ ↗ ↘ ↙

ò ó ô õ ö ō ŏ ő ǒ

! @ £ $ % & * ? >

Typeface
Pyk Medium (2019)

ABCDE
JKLMN
STUVW
ERICA

FGHI
OPQR
XYZ
C

Typeface
Pyk Medium (2019)

Liron Turkenich is a Israeli type and graphic designer. After graduating from Shenkar College of Design in Tel Aviv (B.Des in Visual Communications), she came to the UK to study an MA in Typeface Design at the University of Reading. Her focus is on multilingual typeface design specialising in Hebrew and Amharic.

For her journey to Jerusalem, Makeda took

camels

ማከዳ መልከ ፈደል

Schmuckstücke

סוגים שונים של בשמים וזהב

spices

ወደ ኢየሩሳሌም ስትሄድ የከበሪ ድንጋይᎂመርቆᎂሽቱ

תכשיטים רבים

and precious stones

Typeface
Makeda (2013)

www.lironlavi.com

MÅKËĐÁ haś Ĕxtêêèndëęď Ĺàáâãäåtîñ Šüppòóôõöřt וְגַם נְנְנֶנֶנִיקוּד בְּעִבְרִית

(aʻn£d) — se¥ve\ra$l ¡sϖignʻs! a#n/d ¿p@unc*tua€tiʻo•n? "mˉarks"; fo-r [ev&ery:] «sc∷ript»...

numerals 1934 ⚏⚎⚍⚌ 1825 600

a SET OF SMALL CAPS
And Caps For Really Long German Words

Makeda Regular

Three scripts, ten styles.

Makeda is the first typeface that covers Latin, Hebrew and Amharic (Ethiopic). The three scripts were designed simultaneously in order to allow for mutual influences. The design efforts were put into harmonising the scripts into one coherent family, while preserving their basic traditional structure. A work of gentle balances and fascinating research assisted in the design of the **Makeda** typeface.

Latin Regular

Latin Bold

Latin Black

Latin Italic

Amharic Regular

Hebrew Regular

Amharic Bold

Hebrew Bold

Amharic Black

Hebrew Black

Lynne Yun is a NYC-based type designer who specialises in typography, hand lettering and calligraphy. Previously working for brands such as Apple, Publicis, and Deutsch, Lynne is now a type designer at Monotype and serves as a board member of AIGA NY.

Typeface
Trade Gothic Display

An example of her highly rated works is **Trade Gothic Display**. Based on the popular **Trade Gothic** family, Lynne designed this display family that could compliment the current collection from Monotype. **Trade Gothic Display** 1 & 2 is a series that incorporates layers and would allow for 3-dimensional effects. The first style is an embossed weight with highlights designed to swell and wane, maximising the illusion of the raised surface. The second style is a bevelled weight, which mimics carved letters on a physical surface. This style has a shadow layer and an outline layer so users can pick their own combinations.

@lynneyun
www.lynneyun.com

ABCDEFGHIJKLMNOPQRSTU
VWXYZÀÁÂÃÄÅÆ
ØŒÙÚÛÜ0123456789&!?

ABCDEFGHIJKLMNOPQRSTU
VWXYZÀÁÂÃÄÅÆ
ØŒÙÚÛÜ0123456789&!?

ABCDEFGHIJKLMNOPQRSTU
VWXYZÀÁÂÃÄÅÆ
ØŒÙÚÛÜ0123456789&!?

ABCDEFGHIJKLMNOPQRSTU
VWXYZÀÁÂÃÄÅÆ
ØŒÙÚÛÜ0123456789&!?

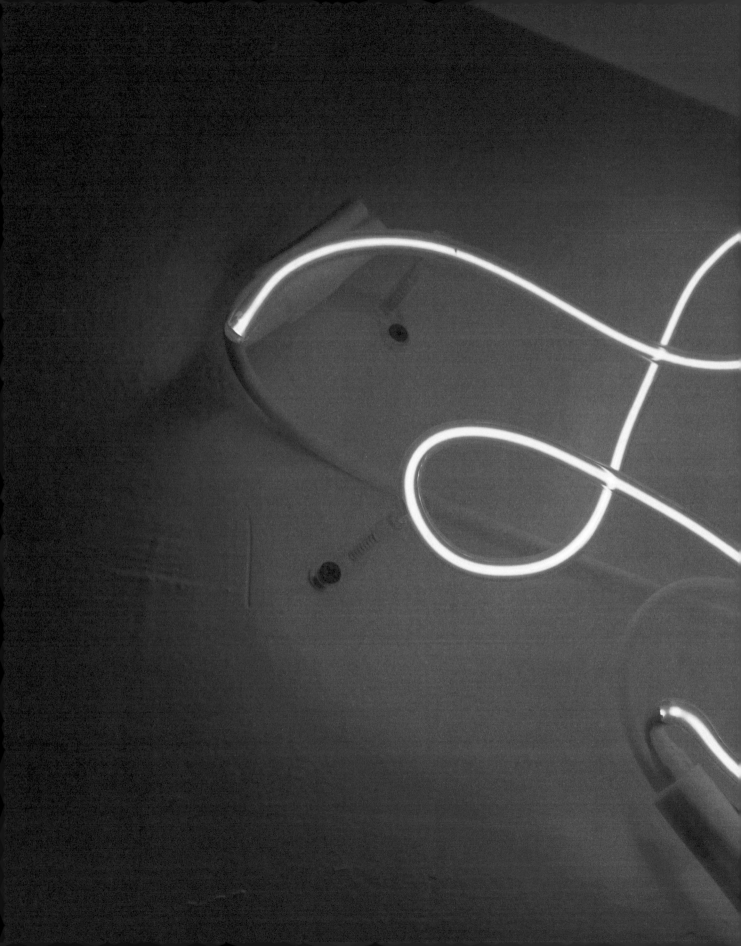

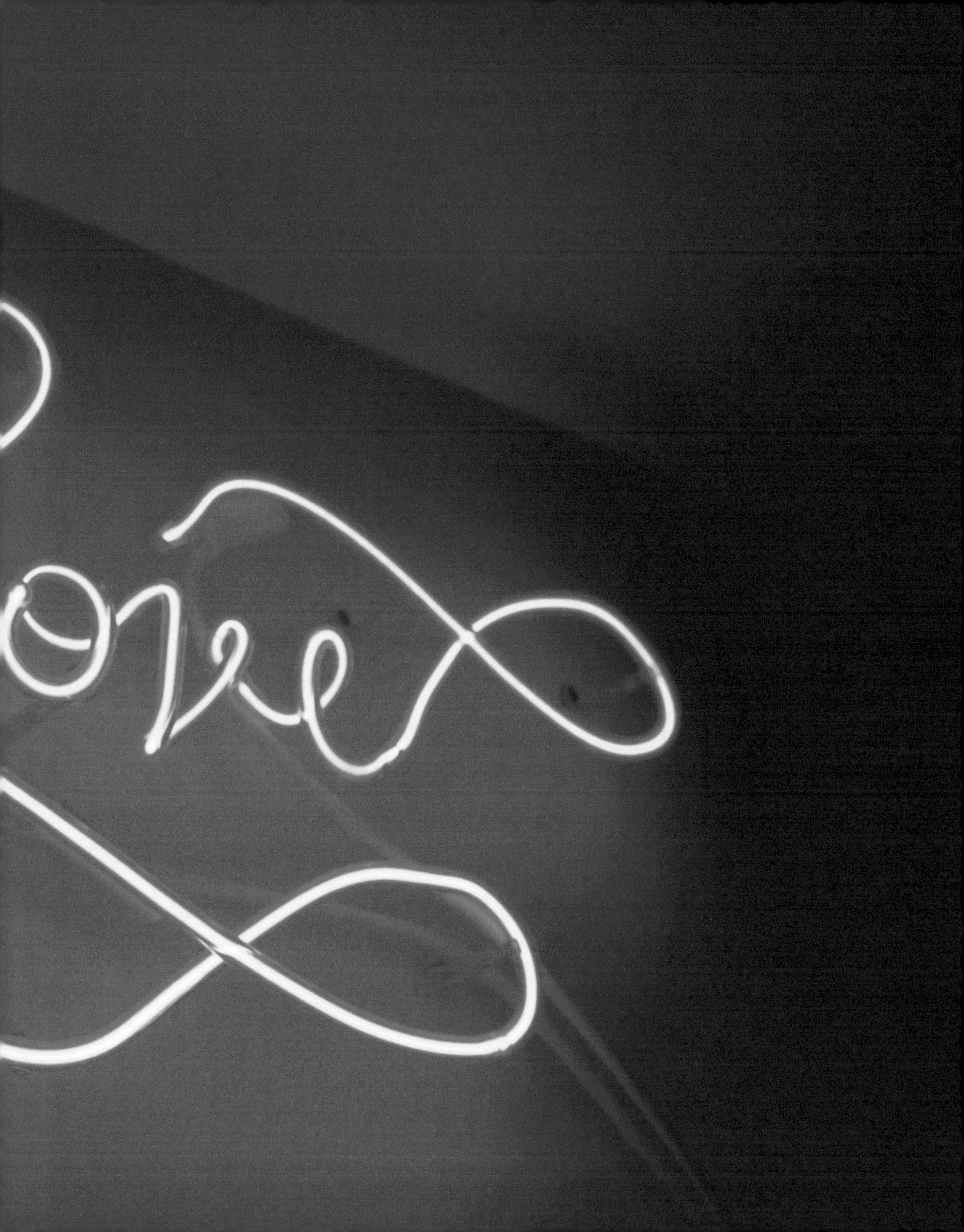

TYPOGRAPHY

Veronica Fuerte / Hey Studio
Shanti Sparrow
Rita Matos
Caterina Bianchini Studio
Marta & Eva Yarza / Yarza Twins
Hui Yeon Hwang
Isabel Urbina Peña
Eugénie Favre & Carole Gautier / My Name is Wendy
Marta Gawin
Marina Chaccur
Marta Cerda
Letitia Lin
Hello this is Kae
Tina Touli
Anastasia Liolio
Tamara Arkatova

Founded by graphic designer
Veronica Fuerte, Hey Studio is
an established Barcelona-based
design studio producing exquisite
creative solutions in the realms
of branding, digital and print.
We interviewed Veronica to find
out her journey of setting up this
prestigious brand and studio.

@heystudio
www.heystudio.es

60th Anniversary Helvetica
(2018)

What inspired you to set up Hey Studio?

As soon as I had finished university it was already clear to me that I wanted to have my own style and my own vision on how to do things. First though, I needed to learn more from other people and studios but after 7 years of working like that I decided to run my own studio. It was something that I personally felt a strong desire to do and was probably because I wanted to express myself more as a creative.

What do you think are the most important elements when setting up an independent studio?

At the beginning, I think the most important thing is take your time. It's best to think properly what you want to do and how you want to do it. The first years you have a lot of energy and drive which is an amazing feeling and something that you should try and keep for as long as you possibly can.

What's the most valuable lesson you've learnt running a studio?

Patience but the most valuable thing is choosing the right people to help you. Not only do they need to be compatible design-wise but also in how they work and how they are as people. When all these things click then you're well on the way.

What are your thoughts on type in the current design industry? How has it changed over the years?

Type design is the factor that has the most history in graphic design and I think it's important to show some respect to its rich past. It is very obvious but technology has an effect on how it is seen and

used. I think typeface design is always about experimenting but what is changing is how it has become more flexible and alive thanks to technology.

What's your favourite typeface or style of type and why?

Neue Unica Haas. It's a mixture of different typefaces I like: Helvetica, Univers and Akzidenz Grotesk.

Can you make any predictions about the future of type?

I think we can now see much more clearly how almost all typefaces are going to evolve. They will keep their essence and their connection to their roots, but they won't be constrained in how they are exposed. There will be more movement, coding will play a bit role as well as continued experimentation. Basically, they will become more alive.

Finally, what has been your favourite project to work on?

It is always difficult to choose just one because with all of them I've learned something - even, or perhaps especially, the bad ones! But maybe because of my relationship with the client and how it turned out, I have a lot of fondness for a project I did for a friend: **Jammy-yummy.**

Shanti Sparrow is an award-winning Australian graphic designer, illustrator, and lecturer. Specialising as a focused conceptual designer within the NGO industry, Shanti focuses on awareness campaigns. Also known as the Queen of Layout, her work is characteristically informed by the grid with refined typography and bold colour choices.

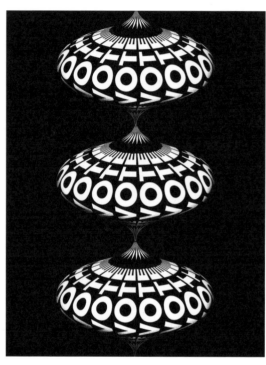

Mind Blown
(2018)

Embracing the simplicity of geometric shapes and lines throughout her work, Shanti creates minimal yet visually striking designs. It was these designs that lead to the designer to be named one of **33 Women Doing Amazing Things in Graphic Design** along with design superstars Paula Sher, Jessica Walsh and Debbie Millman.

The Transform Exhibition identity was developed for the **Shillington School of Design** graduation exhibition. The concept of 'Transform' was inspired by the student journey - from curious observer to passionate designer. Its graphics reflect the transitional stages of change in both abstract elements and typography. The exhibition identity was rolled out internationally in New York, London, Sydney, Manchester, Brisbane and Melbourne campuses.

@shanti_sparrow
www.shantisparrow.com

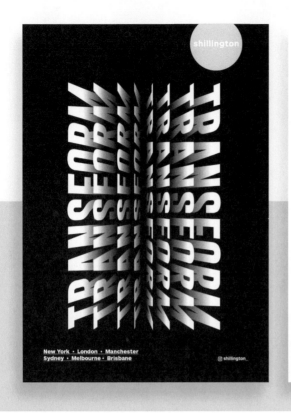

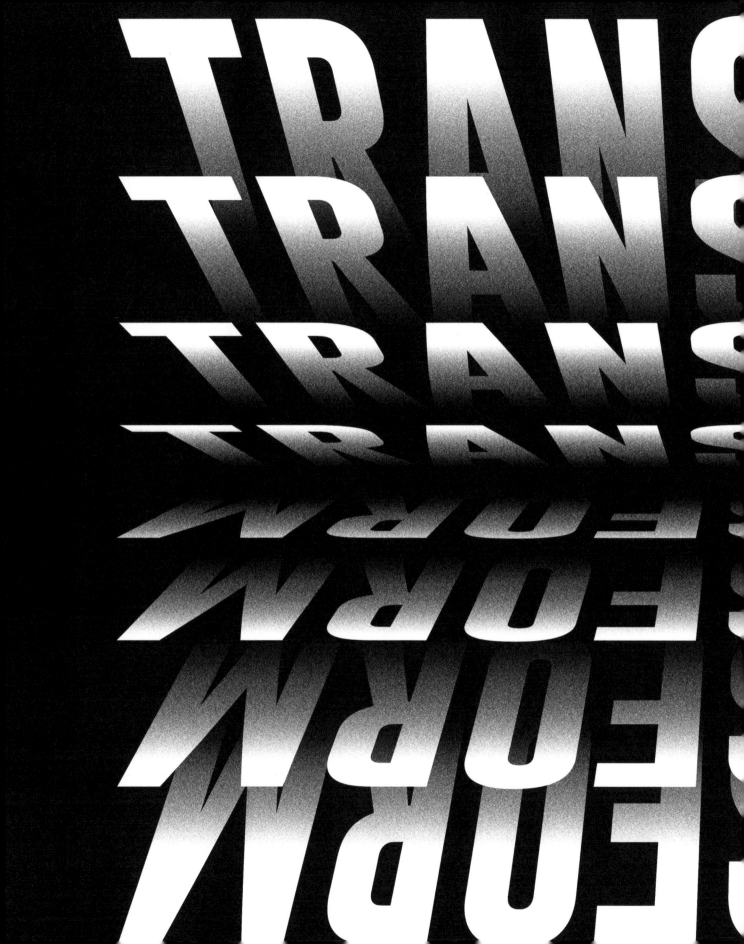

Rita Matos is a Portuguese graphic designer based in Lisbon, specialising in the cultural field. Graduating from Lisbon's Faculty of Fine Arts in 2013 with a Communication Design degree, she shortly after became part of Silvadesigner's studio, where she worked on a wide range of editorial, visual identity and branding projects.

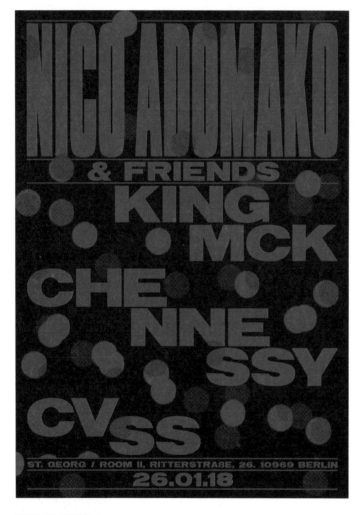

NICO ADOMAKO & FRIENDS (2018)

XXIII is a promotional poster project focused on music collective **XXIII** based in Porto, Portugal. Music brand **XXIII** promotes new electronic sounds and Portuguese creativity and is deeply rooted in urban culture. Rita's style takes the form of a bold typographic aesthetic using large letters and glyphs to create powerful poster graphics.

@aritamatos
www.ritamatos.com

PALOMA BAR SK LI ZER STR. 135, 10999 BERLIN
TICKLISH
IAMNOBODI
THE PERSEVERANCE
BRAT STAR
STICKLE
INAN
LEE STUART
TUAN: ANH
DIANA BOSS
MELIS
HAIZEL
FINGALICK
AND MORE...
NICO ADOMAKO
& FRIENDS
X TINY PIZZA PARTY
8.11

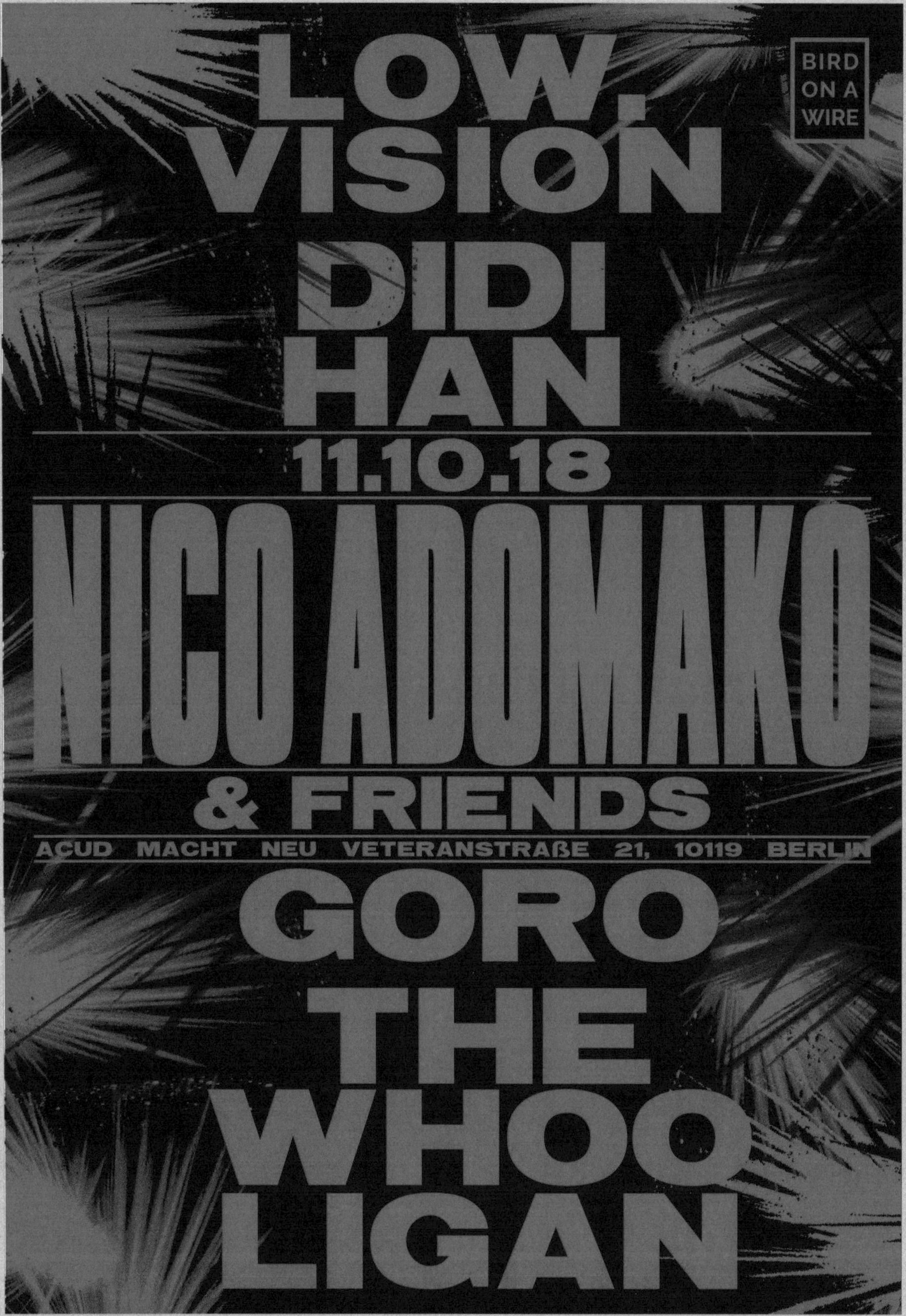
LOW.
VISION
BIRD ON A WIRE
DIDI
HAN
11.10.18
NICO ADOMAKO
& FRIENDS
ACUD MACHT NEU VETERANSTRAßE 21, 10119 BERLIN
GORO
THE
WHOO
LIGAN

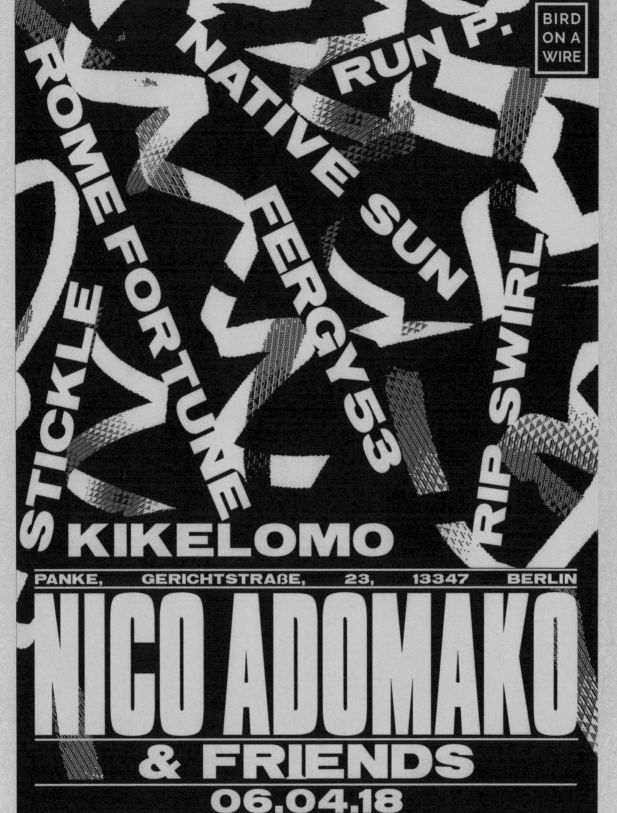

ANI KLANG
DJ JM
BIRD ON A WIRE
TUAN:ANH
QUMASI,
QUAME
17.08.18
NICO ADOMAKO
& FRIENDS
ACUD MACHT NEU VETERANSTRAßE 21, 10119 BERLIN

XXIII W/ MINA
22 SET 18
MAUS HÁBITOS
PORTO

VISUALS BY
メカMECHA

SOB O OLHAR DA...
CORUJA

blastah
torres
baltazar

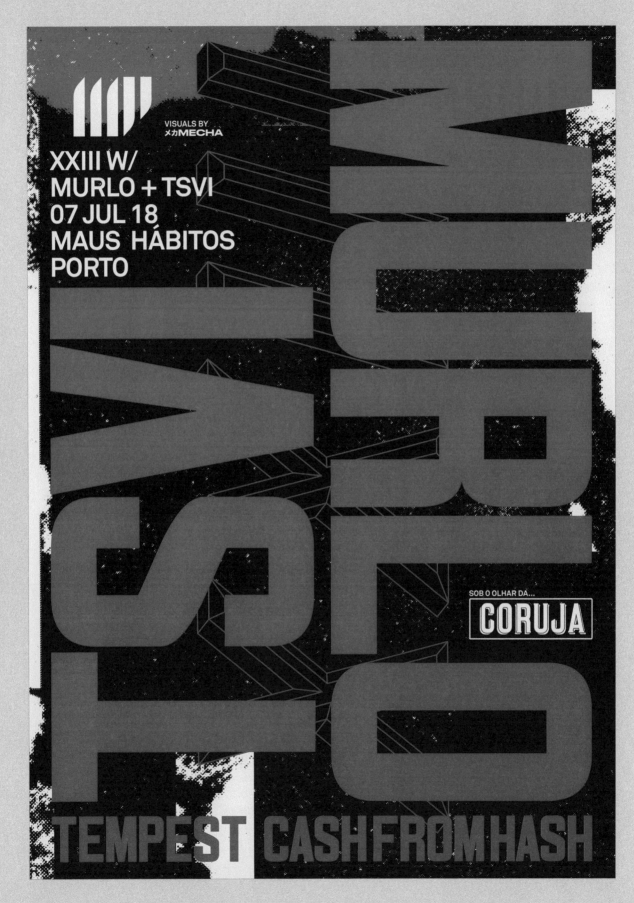

VISUALS BY
メカMECHA

XXIII W/
MURLO + TSVI
07 JUL 18
MAUS HÁBITOS
PORTO

SOB O OLHAR DA...
CORUJA

MURLO

TSVI

TEMPEST CASH FROM HASH

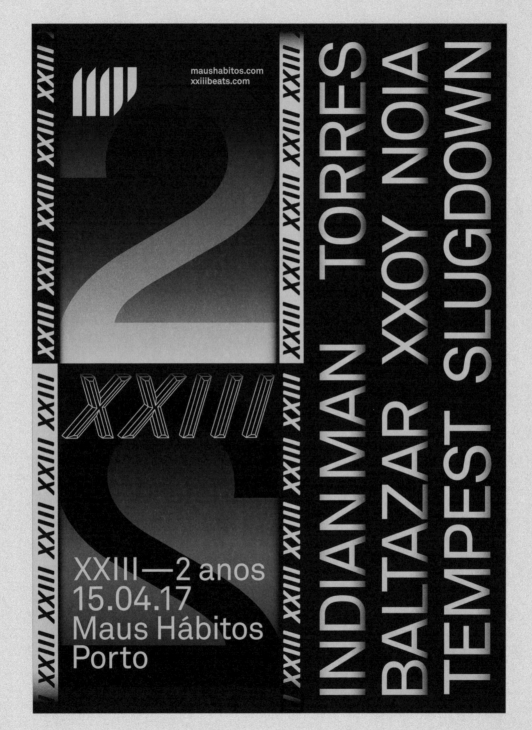

XXIII (2018)

xxiiibeats.com

XXIII — 18.11.17

VISUALS BY
メカMECHA

KLEAR   NL

JAËL

Maus
Hábitos
Porto

XXIII   PT

T
O
R
R
E
S

P   T

B
E
N
T

BOKO   BOKO,   UK

TASH LC

full crate

noia

ben

torres

XXIII
3 ANOS:
FULL
CRATE

14.04.18
MAUS
HÁBITOS
PORTO

VISUALS BY メカMECHA

RITA MATOS

032

FSGREEN

XXIII

XXIII w/ FS Green
26.05.17
Hardclub – Porto

10€

ENTRADA
ENTRADA

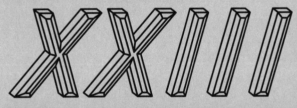

KKING KONG

BALTAZAR   CASH FROM HASH

JUVENIL ANGÚSTIA
CASH FROM HASH
TAKEOVER
TORRES BALTAZAR
XXOY

XXIII
TAKEOVER
19 JAN
23H
PÉROLA
NEGRA
PORTO

CONSUMO MÍNIMO
OBRIGATÓRIO: 5€ CONSUMÍVEIS

VISUALS BY
メカMECHA

PÉROLA
NEGRA

Based in London, Caterina Bianchini is an independent and multi-award winning art and design studio.
Type is strongly at the centre of founder Caterina's work for clients such as Red Bull, Adidas, Levi's, Nike and many other established brands.

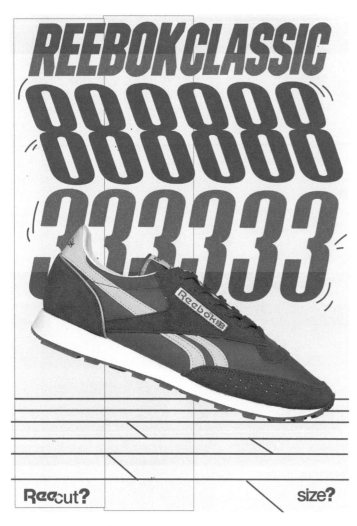

Reebok Originals Campaign
(2018)

Caterina often produces hand-drawn type for her designs, a talent that she's nurtured her entire career and has been noticed by established platforms such as **It's Nice That**. Pictured right and above are example posters created as part of a campaign for the **Reebok Originals** re-released 80s track shoe in summer 2018. Each poster encapsulates the concept of movement, particularly focusing on the theme of Bounciness relating directly to the sole of the track shoe and the Astro Turf running track. Bespoke typography was created and can be seen in various formats across the campaign. Naturally, they match the neon colour palette of the shoe. The final project was released across the UK and installed in-store in all Size shoe stores across the country.

@caterinabianchinistudio
www.caterinabianchini.com

WE WORK
CREATOR AWARDS

WE WORK
CREATOR AWARDS

BERLIN

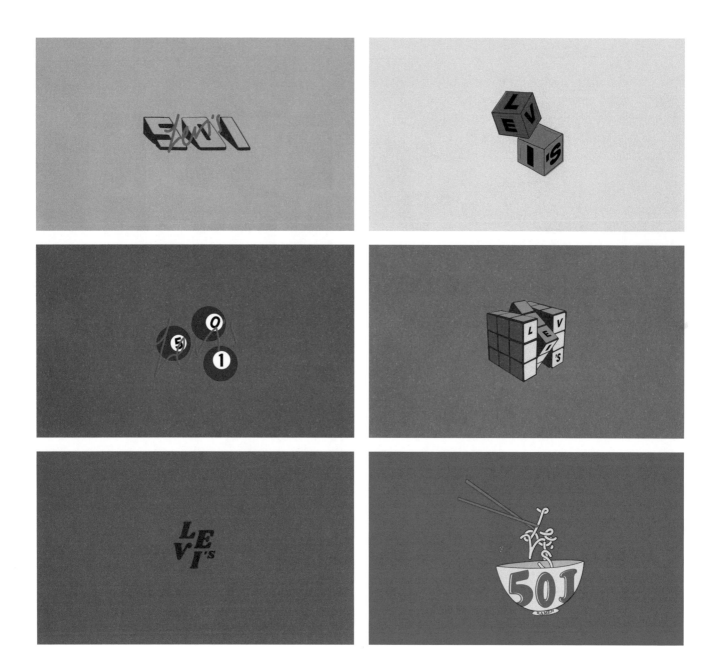

Levi's Logos

Commissioned by fashion house **Levi's,** Caterina
incorporates additional examples of her brilliant
custom typography skills by re-imagining the **Levi's**
logo. By completely removing it from its well known
red and white, bold graphic, the designs showcase
illustrative lock ups coupled with bespoke typography,
giving the logo a completely new look.

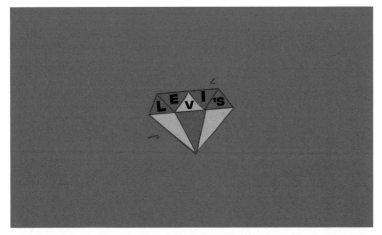

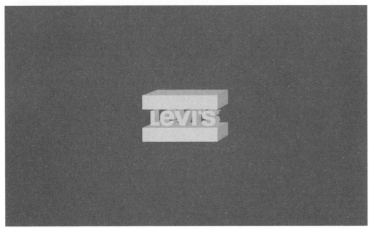

Twin-sibling duo Eva and Marta Yarza make up London-based graphic design studio Yarza Twins. They combine creativity, concept and strategy to create bold high impact typographic projects for the likes of Adidas, Converse and many other clients.

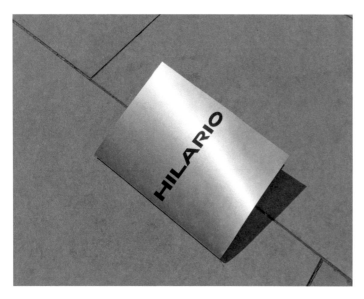

Hilario Typeface
(2017)

Among their design achievements, last year they were awarded a prestigious **D&AD** Pencil in Packaging Design 2018 as well as being 1 of the 15 most exciting designers under 30 named by **Print Magazine** 2016. They have also been nominated for "best creative concept" at International **Fashion Film festival** 2017 for their film for fashion designer May Gidah. A list of brilliant typographic projects include a bold poster campaign for **Adidas London**; a collaboration with **It's Nice That** with an artistic context; **Hilario**, an extended bold **Neue Grotesk typeface**; identity design for music band **Supermeganada**; and finally, redesigning concept and creativity print magazine **Neo2**.

@yarza_twins
www.yarzatwins.com

As part of their design commission for **Adidas London** the **Yarza Twins** created a series of bold typographic posters to mark the opening of their **Adidas** Football Creator Base in London, a pop-up event space that celebrated the start of the World Cup 2018. Using custom large scale typography and bright colours the team constructed a series of motivational word combinations and phrases to feature as the main component.

Converse Poster
(2018)

NEO2

Enero — Febrero 2019 / Spain 5€

Nº 162

Tendencias
King Jedet
Diseño Gráfico

Magnus Mästberg
Meesha Roseg

162
Ene
—Feb
2019

Canarias: 4,20 € / PT: 5 € / IT: 4,90 €
FR: 6,50 € / TW: 4,90 € / UK: 5,99 £

9 771138 562005   00162

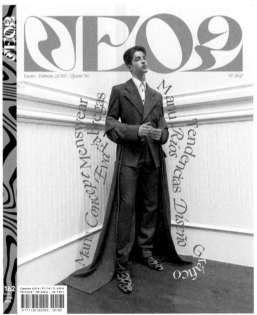

Neo2 is a Spanish magazine aiming to share with the world the latest art and design trends and the newest national talent through fashion, music, art and culture. The redesign produced by **Yarza Twins** included the dramatic logotype as well as the general guidelines for the magazine. The playfulness of the logo's letter forms represents the fluidity of the arts and how they evolve gradually over time.

Originally from Seoul, Hui Yeon works across print, identities and editorial design with her outputs often incorporating both 2D and 3D typographic elements. You can find rotating logos, holographic imagery and futuristic tones and heavy game references throughout her work.

STU Identity
(2018)

@huiyeonh
www.huiyeonh.com

Græi   Græi   Græi   Græi   Græi

AS URBAN MATERIALS

THE PROTECTIVE COLOR

AS URBAN MATERIALS

THE PROTECTIVE COLOR

Græi   Græi   Græi   Græi   Græi

GRAEI Poster Series
(2017)

HAULIN' ON
TRUCKING
GAME
THE VIRTUAL
BIGSLAB
SIMULATION
TRUCKER UNION®
stu®

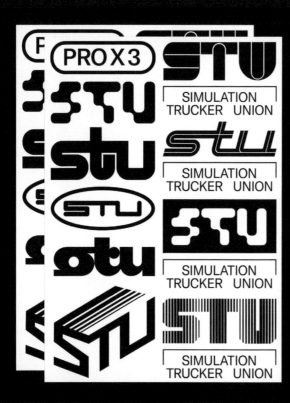

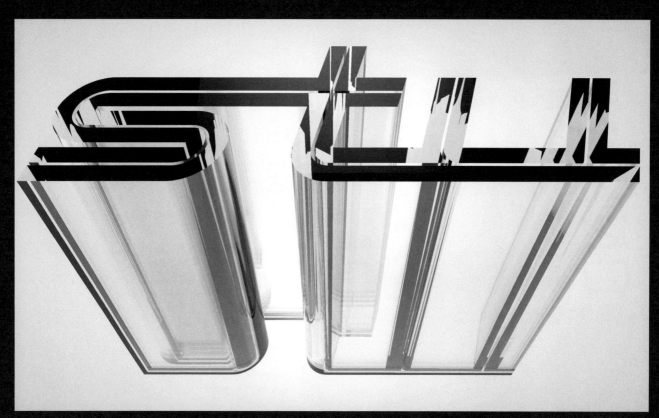

INNING AND

Seung-Taik Hwang   Chief Executive

T   + 02 543 5168
           + 02 541 4832
F   + 02 543 5169
E   Inningandst@hotmail.com

INNING AND

::

INNING AND
is not only a typical textile distributor/an agent, but also a unique creator and a trailblazer in coping with fashion makers between Korean and Italian fashion field. Inning has remained open and devoted to both its suppliers and its top tier customers since beginning.

INNING AND
has never made a promise to renounce the use of its wide variety of curiosity and reserve the option of taking all necessary means in bridging the gap between fashion fantasies and real-world demands.

INNING AND CORP.
SINCE 1996

::

STU Identity
(2018)

Hui Yeon developed the identity graphics, which also featured as part of her Thesis at **California Institute of the Arts**, for **STU** (Simulation Trucker Union), a virtual labour union for truck simulation game users. Hui Yeon designed the union's visual identity and online promotion graphics both of which were inspired by seeing game users attaching actual labour union logos onto their truck skin to boost the overall team spirit as virtual truckers.

HUI YEON HWANG   035

Isabel is a Brooklyn NY-based multidisciplinary artist originally from Venezuela. Isabel runs her own studio in New York focusing on everything typographic. One of Isabel's proud accomplishments includes being named a New Visual Artist (15 under 30) by PRINT Magazine in 2015. In her spare time she teaches, speaks at conferences, draws zines and runs Yes, Equal, a database of women in the creative fields.

Girlboss Rally. Environmental Graphics for Girlboss.
Commissioned by: Makeout NYC (2018)

Custom lettering for Dirty Bandit's 10 Commandments
(2018)

BUZZFEED 'Who Is She?' Lettering
(2018)

@bellera
www.isabelurbinapena.com

ISABEL URBINA PEÑA

RELEASE YOURSELF FROM WHAT DOES NOT SERVE YOU

Girlboss Instagram Material
(2018)

Girlboss Instagram Material
(2018)

My Name is Wendy is a Paris-based studio made up graphic designers, Carole Gautier and Eugenie Favre. They create high-impact, bold graphic solutions utlising type as one of the main visual elements.

Hohe Luft / Philosophy Magazine
Hamburg Issue 1/19
Typeface: Greta Lührs ll

Featured in Philosphy magazine Hamburg issue, **My Name is Wendy** produced typographic artwork for an article about saying "Nein". The word "No" can equally express Autonomy, Unwissen (ignorance), Widerstand (resistance) or Verachtung (contempt) and it was the creative team's job to produce a visual for it. Getting the walls to talk - literally. Such was the poetic aspiration of the **Etant donné un mur** project initiated by social landlord Alcéane which was buoyed by the festivals Une Saison Graphique and Le Goût des Autres in Le Havre. 22 building walls had a complete makeover, drawing inspiration from literature and the graphic arts. Works were specially commissioned from Benoît Duteurtre, Camélia Jordana, Maylis de Kerangal, Céline Minard, Marie Nimier, Christophe Ono-dit-Biot, Véronique Ovaldé, Joy Sorman, François Vallejo or Valérie Zenatti, selected by the festival Le Goût des Autres.

To transform the walls, graphic artists Betty Bone, Erich Brechbühl, Virgile Laguin, **My Name Is Wendy**, Richard Niessen, Laura Kopf, Damien Poulain, R2 Design, Grégoire Romanet, Pierre di Sciullio and Twice, were selected by A Graphic Season. The purpose of the exhibition was to show a way for those who live in and around the city's walls to regain a sense of belonging while also learning another facet of the place they call home.

Oposing page: A summer in le Havre / 500 years - 22 walls / 10 authors / 11 graphic artists. Urban exhibition.
Type: Valérie Zenatti

@mynameiswendystudio
www.mynameiswendy.fr

WIDERSTAND

VERACHTUNG

VERACH
TUNG

UNWI
SSEN

AUTONOMIE

WIDERSTAND

UNWISSEN

VERACHTUNG

UNWISSEN

WIDERSTAND

AUTO
NOMIE

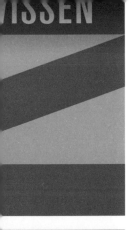

Hohe Luft / Philosophy Magazine
Hamburg Issue 1/19
Typeface: Greta Lührs ll

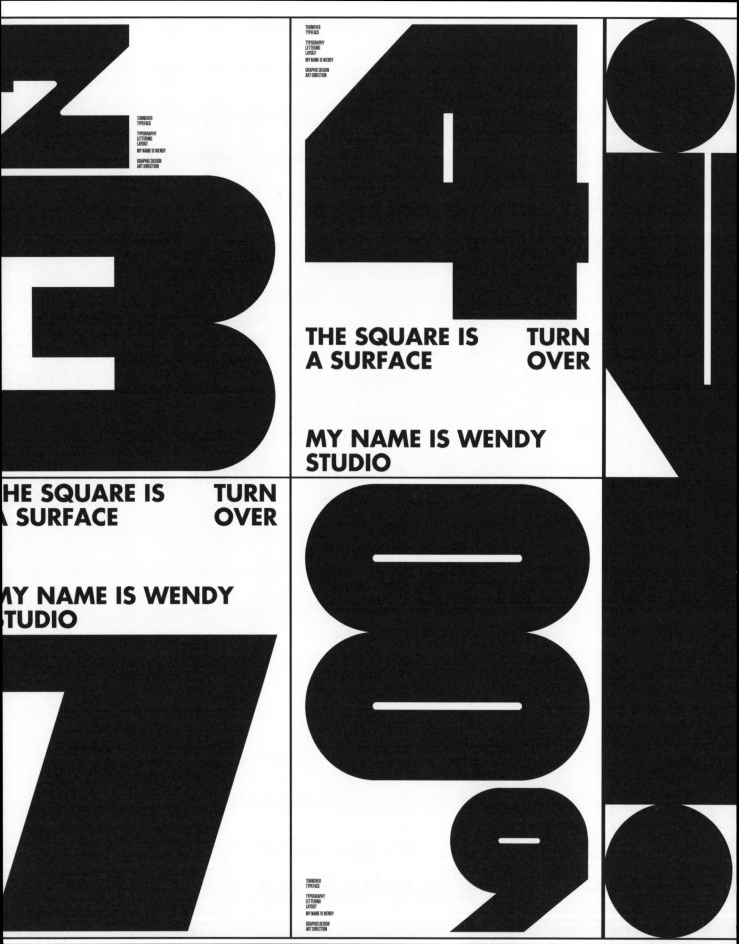

TURNOVER
TYPEFACE

TYPOGRAPHY
LETTERING
LAYOUT
MY NAME IS WENDY

GRAPHIC DESIGN
ART DIRECTION

TURNOVER
TYPEFACE

TYPOGRAPHY
LETTERING
LAYOUT
MY NAME IS WENDY

GRAPHIC DESIGN
ART DIRECTION

THE SQUARE IS   TURN
A SURFACE   OVER

MY NAME IS WENDY
STUDIO

THE SQUARE IS   TURN
A SURFACE   OVER

MY NAME IS WENDY
STUDIO

TURNOVER
TYPEFACE

TYPOGRAPHY
LETTERING
LAYOUT
MY NAME IS WENDY

GRAPHIC DESIGN
ART DIRECTION

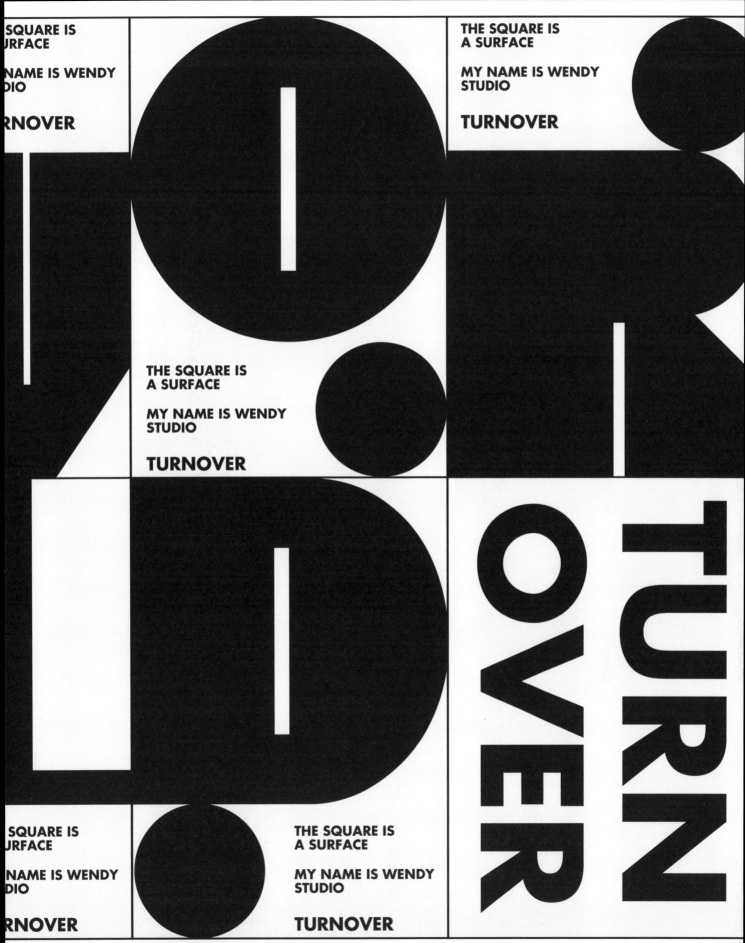

THE SQUARE IS
A SURFACE

MY NAME IS WENDY
STUDIO

TURNOVER

THE SQUARE IS
A SURFACE

MY NAME IS WENDY
STUDIO

TURNOVER

THE SQUARE IS
A SURFACE

MY NAME IS WENDY
STUDIO

TURNOVER

TURN
OVER

Typeface
Turnover (2019)

Turnover is both a typeface and a series of bold shapes and signs. Constructed on the basis of square, **Turnover** is a fixed width typeface enhancing the balance between the high contrast of black and white. Due to being based on the simple grid, it allows for the designer to create bold, high impact typographic layouts.

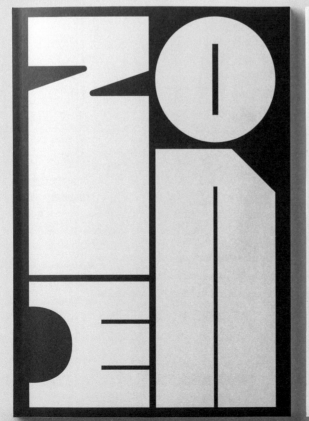

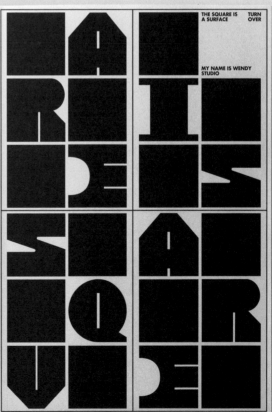

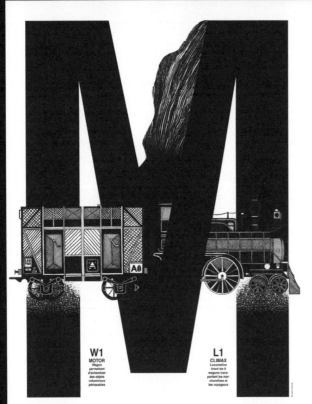

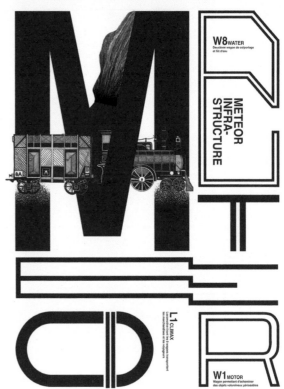

W1
MOTOR
Wagon
permettant
d'acheminer
des objets
volumineux
périssables

L1
CLIMAX
Locomotive
tirant les 9
wagons trans-
portant les mar-
chandises et
les voyageurs

W8WATER
Deuxième wagon de colportage
et fût d'eau

METEOR
INFRA-
STRUCTURE

L1 CLIMAX
Locomotive tirant les 9 wagons transportant
les marchandises et les voyageurs

W1 MOTOR
Wagon permettant d'acheminer
des objets volumineux périssables

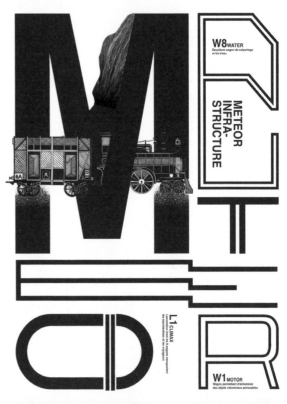

W1
MOTOR
Wagon
permettant
d'acheminer
des objets
volumineux
périssables

L1
CLIMAX
Locomotive
tirant les 9
wagons trans-
portant les mar-
chandises et
les voyageurs

W8WATER
Deuxième wagon de colportage
et fût d'eau

METEOR
INFRA-
STRUCTURE

L1 CLIMAX
Locomotive tirant les 9 wagons transportant
les marchandises et les voyageurs

W1 MOTOR
Wagon permettant d'acheminer
des objets volumineux périssables

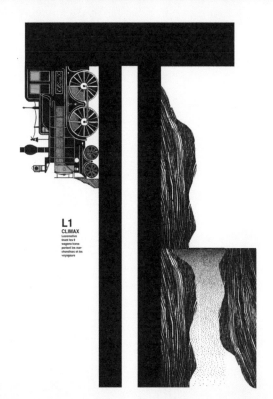

METEOR
INFRA-
STRUCTURE

L1
CLIMAX
Locomotive
tirant les 9
wagons de mar-
chandises et de
voyageurs

W1 MOTOR
Wagon permettant d'acheminer des objets
volumineux périssables

W2 LET'S GO
Wagon frigorifique pour les denrées et les liquides

L1 CLIMAX
Locomotive tirant les 9 wagons transportant
les marchandises et les voyageurs

W7 ROSSYIA
Wagon transportant l'eau tirée de la rivière

W2
LET'S GO
Wagon frigorifi-
que pour les
denrées et les
liquides

W7
ROSSYIA
Wagon transpor-
tant l'eau tirée
de la rivière

W1
MOTOR
Wagon d'objets
volumineux pé-
rissables

L1
CLIMAX
Locomotive
tirant les 9
wagons trans-
portant les mar-
chandises et les
voyageurs

L1 CLIMAX
Locomotive tirant les 9 wagons transportant
les marchandises et les voyageurs

METEOR
INFRA-
STRUCTURE

W2. LET'S GO
Wagon frigorifique pour les denrées et les liquides

W1 MOTOR
Wagon permettant d'acheminer
des objets volumineux périssables

Within Magazine
gowithin.co

Graphic Design
My name is wendy

The designer's guide
to meetings where
all voices are heard
By Julie Zhuo

WITHIN

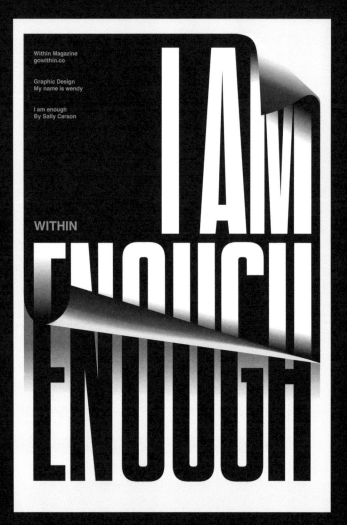

Within Magazine
gowithin.co

Graphic Design
My name is wendy

I am enough
By Sally Carson

Within Magazine / San Francisco
(2018)

Within Magazine exists to do three things: challenge the status quo of leadership in design and technology, share practical wisdom for creating environments where all people thrive, and amplify stories of more diverse leaders. More than a magazine, **Within** is a community that is driving design towards a more diverse and inclusive future. **My Name is Wendy** created these powerful typographical compositions for articles stating, "we are self-identifying women who have come together to share, learn, and reinvent. Real change may be born of us, but it will take more than us".

I AM ENOUGH

Graphic Design My Name is Wendy

I am enough
By Sally Carson

Whitin Magazine gowithin.co

I am enough
By Sally Carson

WITHIN

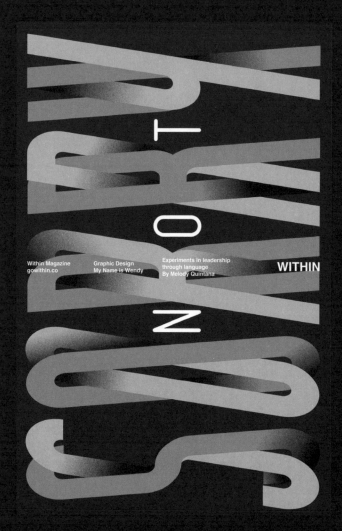

Within Magazine
gowithin.co

Graphic Design
My Name is Wendy

Experiments in leadership
through language
By Melody Quintana

WITHIN

ES

PAC

NOTES EN VUE DU LIVRE

CE BLOG NE PEUT DONC AUCUNEMENT FAIRE UN CARRÉ QUE DE FAÇADE, EN VOYANT LE DOS, PAR EXEMPLE, SOIT DEBOUT SOIT COUCHÉ—MAIS IL NE L'AURA PAS EN PROFONDEUR OÙ—EN CE QUI QUAND ON LE CONSIDÈRE D'EN FACE, DEVIENDRA ÉPAISSEUR (RAPPORT DE L'ÉPAISSEUR DU LIVRE ET SA LARGEUR PAR DEUX FOIS COUCHÉ OU DU DEBOUT D'OÙ LA SIGNALER D'OR—ELLE RESTE LA MÊME TRAIT C'UN EN TRACER EN ÉPAISSEUR ET LARGEUR DONNÉE AUSSI EXACTEMENT AUSSI SERRÉE QUE POSSIBLE.

IL FAUDRA QUE CES SOI LIVRES VOL. SOIENT LES MÊMES—MAIS DIFFÉREMMENT SCRUTÉS—(L   L OU L   L ?)
POUR ÉTABLIR UNE IDENTITÉ
L'ÉCRITURE ÉTANT DONNÉE DEUX FOIS,
N'AYANT D'AUTRE BUT QUE DE MONTRER
LA RAPPORTS SCIENTIFIQUES—DÉCOUVERTE CE LIVRE DE LA VALEUR
FIXER UN PRIX ETC. MAIS PAR CELA MÊME N'IMPRIMANT À
L'AUTEUR

E

DE

L

ECT

U

RE

S. MALLARMÉ

Studio My Name is Wendy

ESPACE DE LECTURE

DIVA-GATIONS
"LE LIVRE, EXPANSION TOTALE DE LA LETTRE, DOIT D'ELLE TIRER, DIRECTEMENT, UNE MOBILITÉ ET SPACIEUX, PAR CORRESPONDANCES, INSTITUER UN JEU, ON NE SAIT, QUI CONFIRME LA FICT"
S.MALLARMÉ

TRANSCRIPTION DU FAUNE
PERDRE
LAISSER
LAISSER
BRISER

S.MALLARMÉ
QUI VOUDRAIS UN CARACTÈRE ASSEZ SOBRE, QUI S'ADAPTÂT À LA CONVERSATION DES VERS, MAIS DE L'AIRE ENTRE LES VERS, AFIN QU'IL SE DÉTACHENT BIEN LES UNS DES AUTRES, CE QUI EST NÉCESSAIRE ENCORE AVEC LEUR CONVERSATION,
P.MENDÈS

ES

PA
C
E

DE
LEC
TU
RE

S.MALLARMÉ

Studio My Name is Wendy

Marta Gawin is a multidisciplinary Polish graphic designer specialising in visual identity, communication design, exhibition design, and editorial design. Gawin's design approach is conceptual, logical and content-driven. She treats graphic design as a field of visual research and formal experiments.

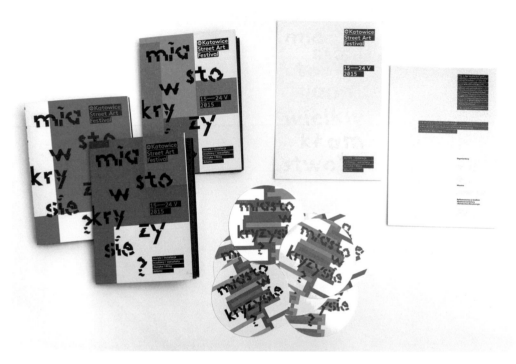

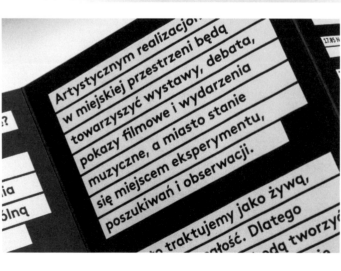

Katowice Street Art Festival
Design Identity (2018)

Poland is internationally known for its large-scale advertising and poster design with a long, lauded tradition of graphic art. **Katowice Street Art Festival** gathers some of the greatest local and international street artists. For its design identity in 2018, Marta created a colourful fluorescent colour palette with fractured typographic letter forms for the promotional flyers, stickers and other marketing materials.

www.gawin.design
www.behance.net/martagawin

228

Marina Chaccur holds a BA (Hons) Design degree, an MA in Graphic Design from the London College of Communication and an MA in Type and Media from the Koninklijke Academie van Beeldende Kunsten. Throughout her career, Marina has constantly been involved in conferences, lectures, workshops and exhibitions worldwide, serving as a board member for Association Typographique Internationale from 2010-2016.

Construction of 'Wet Paint' project
(2015)

Wet Paint is a typographic lettering poster developed for **"Mostra Aberta de Letrismo Contemporâneo"**, an exhibition from 18/07 to 08/08/2015 at Casa SinLogo in São Paulo. Its inspiration originates from the signs made to identify surfaces that had been recently painted. This combined with Marina's personal desire to explore the washi tape as a tool for drawing letters.

@mchaccur
www.marinachaccur.design

Marta Cerda is a Graphic Designer from Barcelona, currently based in Amsterdam. At the end of 2008, after working in agencies and studios between Barcelona and Munich, she won the ADC Young Guns and decided to found her own studio.

BSIDE

_Goin' Wild

BSIDE Book
(A special guide to Barcelona and the OFFF festival,
edited by Atelier.)

Yes! Type treatments for
agency: W+K (Amsterdam)

@martacerda
www.martacerda.com

232

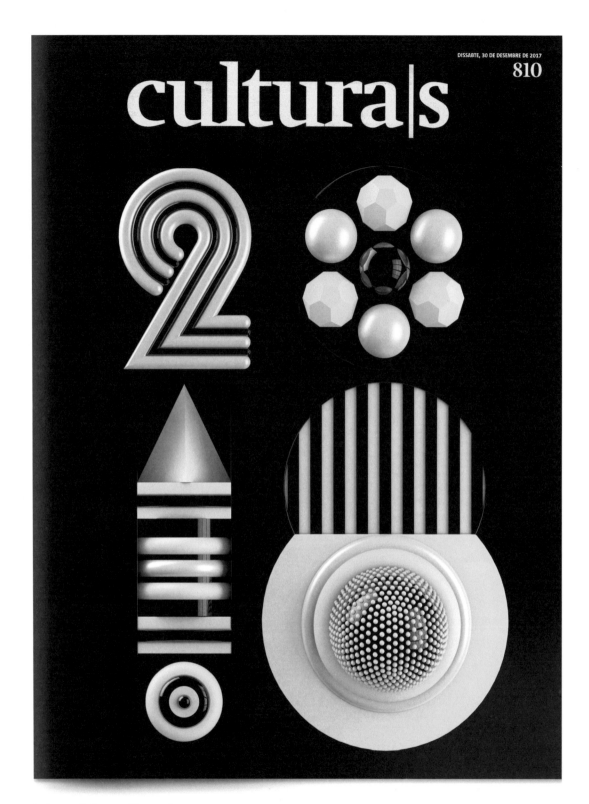

La Vanguardia Typographic cover La
Vanguardia

The Shape of Things

PINSTRIPED, PLAID, DOUBLE-BREASTED, OR CORDUROY,
A PERFECTLY TAILORED SUIT IN A BUY-NOW, KEEP-FOREVER
NEUTRAL IS THIS SEASON'S BEST WAY TO MAKE A
SEXY STATEMENT (THAT'S SURPRISINGLY EASY TO PULL OFF)

Photographs by Jason Kibbler

Amilna (left) in Tibi blazer, $495,
and pants, $375;
tibi.com.
Dries Van Noten
shirt, $310;
saksfifthavenue
.com. Altuzarra
flats, $795;
barneys.com.
Charlene in Polo
Ralph Lauren
blazer, $598,
and pants, $345;
ralphlauren.com.
Dries Van Noten
shoes, $640;
barneys.com.
Nina earring
(worn as brooch),
$15 per pair;
ninashoes.com.
Panthère de Cartier
watch, $4,600;
cartier.com.
Shinola bracelet,
$450; shinola.com.

Fashion Editor:
Jordan Bickham

Vans Old Skool
sneakers, $65; vans.com.
Vinetta checked trousers,
price upon request;
madagproersd.com
and vinetta.it. We Love
Colors socks, $6.50;
welovecolors.com.
Opposite page, from far
left: Pierre Hardy
sliders, $575;
pierrehardy.com.
Alejandro Alonso Rojas
Eleonora polo, $650;
alejandroalonsorojas
.com. Tibi Bianca
cropped pants, $495;
tibi.com. Gola Tennis
Mark Cox trainers, $65;
golausa.com. PH5
Vanessa peplum round-
neck pullover, $189;

Sneak Attack

A CROP OF NEW KICKS ADDS THE PERFECT TOMBOY TOUCH

Photographs by Seiji Fujimori

Lettering for GOOP
Magazine

Letitia Lin is a visual designer based in Taiwan. Focusing on graphic design, branding, key visual, typography, packaging and web design, Letitia's work is characterised by experimental Chinese typography fused with a limited colour palette.

Experimental Chinese Typography Poster Series

Through combining four music styles with four manifestations of font design (hand-writing, transformation, decorative art and original form), and in addition to studying the music-related visual case in the Chinese music market, Letitia's typographic works were applied to four music album singles. Through various techniques, the music album presents the beauty and the times of Chinese characters by rearranging and redesigning the regular pattern of the strokes of traditional Chinese characters containing the concept of aesthetics. It also makes use of different typographic elements and techniques to construct the experimental visual works.

www.behance.net/letitiaO

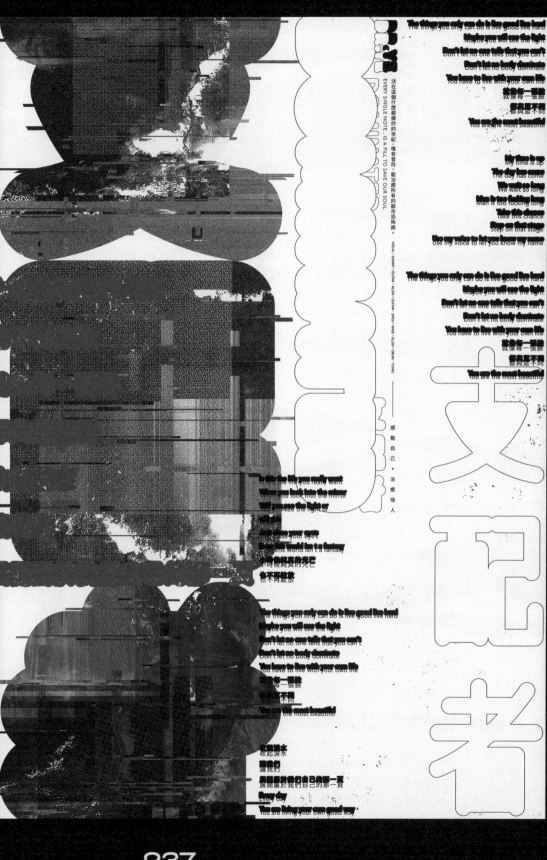

The things you only can do is live good live hard
Maybe you will see the light
Don't let no one tells that you can't
Don't let no body dominate
You have to live with your own life
就像每一張臉
都與眾不同
卻與眾不同
You are the most beautiful

My time is up
The day has come
We wait so long
Man is too fucking long
Take this chance
Step on that stage
Use my voice to let you know my name

The things you only can do is live good live hard
Maybe you will see the light
Don't let no one tells that you can't
Don't let no body dominate
You have to live with your own life
就像每一張臉
都與眾不同
卻與眾不同
You are the most beautiful

Is this the life you really want
When you look into the mirror
Will you see the light or
只看見
Just close your eyes
Maybe this world isn't a fantasy
你時候候純真的先已
也不再綻放

The things you only can do is live good live hard
Maybe you will see the light
Don't let no one tells that you can't
Don't let no body dominate
You have to live with your own life
就像每一張臉
卻與眾不同
You are the most beautiful

收起淚水
朋友們
展開屬於我們自己的那一頁
Every day
You are living your own good way

活在這個什麼都爆炸的世紀，唯有音符，能治癒所有的都市恐怖病。

EVERY SINGLE NOTE, IS A PILL TO SAVE OUR SOUL.

—— 感動自己 · 治癒他人

VOCAL · DANNY / GUITAR · ALLEN / GUITAR · SHOU / BASS · ELLEN / DRUM · TOMO

支配者

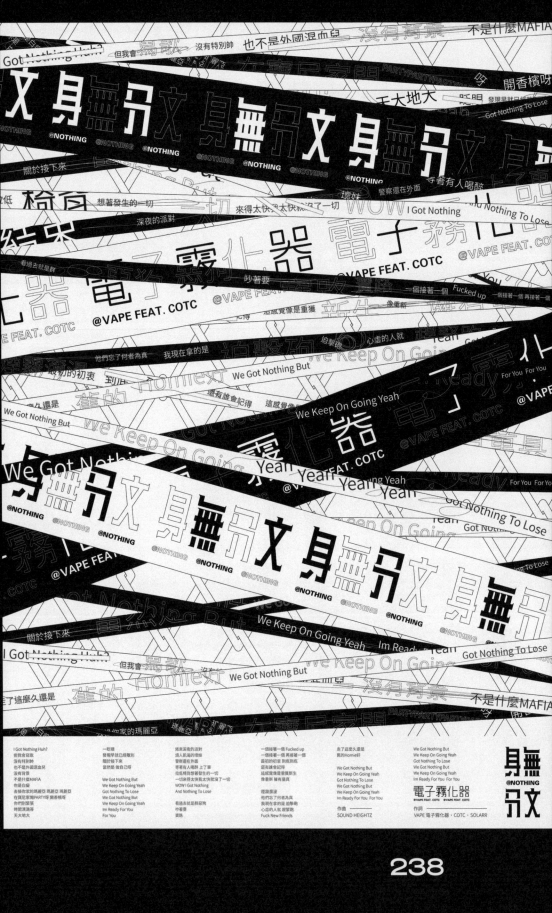

I Got Nothing Huh?
你我會寫歌
沒有特別帥
也不是外國混血兒
沒有背景
不是什麼MAFIA
但是白髮
看操你家的瑪麗亞 瑪麗亞 瑪麗亞
在我玩完PARTY得 開香檳啦
時間消逝著
天大地大

一叹嘛
發覺早就已經實別
關於接下來
當然是 做自己啐

We Got Nothing But
We Keep On Going Yeah
Got Nothing To Lose
We Got Nothing But
We Keep On Going Yeah
Im Ready For You
For You

姓來深夜的派對
混入氯淹的嘴唇
警察還在外面
等著有人喝醉 上了車
拉低帽簷想著發生的一切
一切來得太快就沒了一切
WOW I Got Nothing
And Nothing To Lose
摆踵蹊溜
地的忘了何者為真
我現在拿的是 趕緊跑
看過去就是群星閃
吵著要
資訊

一個接著一個 Fucked up
一個接著一個 再接著一個
最初的初衷 到底剩到底
還有誰會記得
這感覺像是重獲新生
像象新 擁有資真

走了這麼久還是
舊的Homie好

We Got Nothing But
We Keep On Going Yeah
Got Nothing To Lose
We Keep On Going Yeah
Im Ready For You For You

Fuck New Friends

作曲 ———
SOUND HEIGHTZ

We Got Nothing But
We Keep On Going Yeah
Got Nothing To Lose
We Got Nothing But
Im Ready For You For You

電子霧化器
@VAPE FEAT. COTC @VAPE FEAT. COTC

作詞 ———
VAPE 電子霧化器・COTC・SOLARR

無
@NOTHING
分文

LETITIA LIN

042

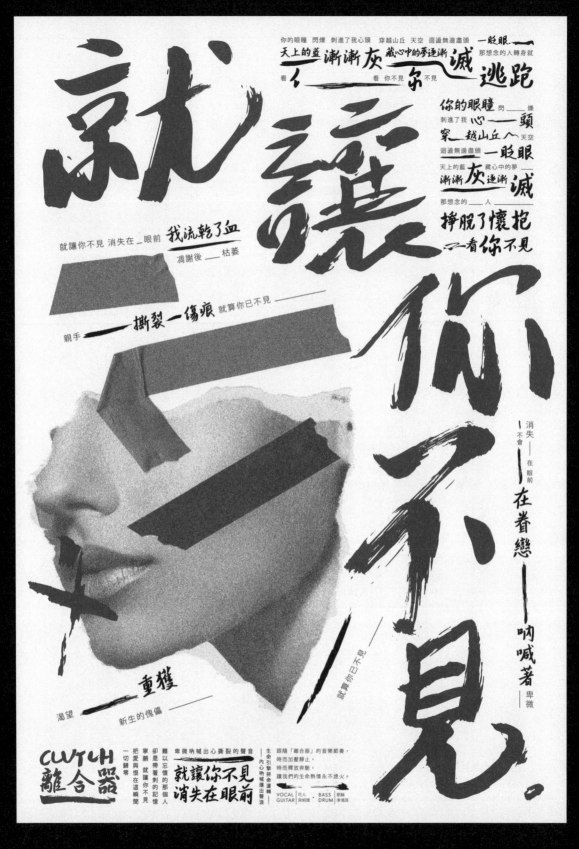

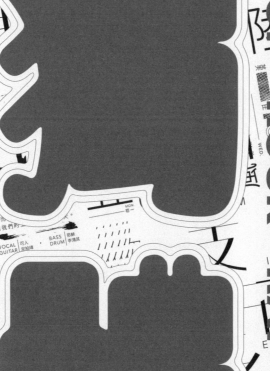

七月記事

EDISON

———

宋柏緯

07

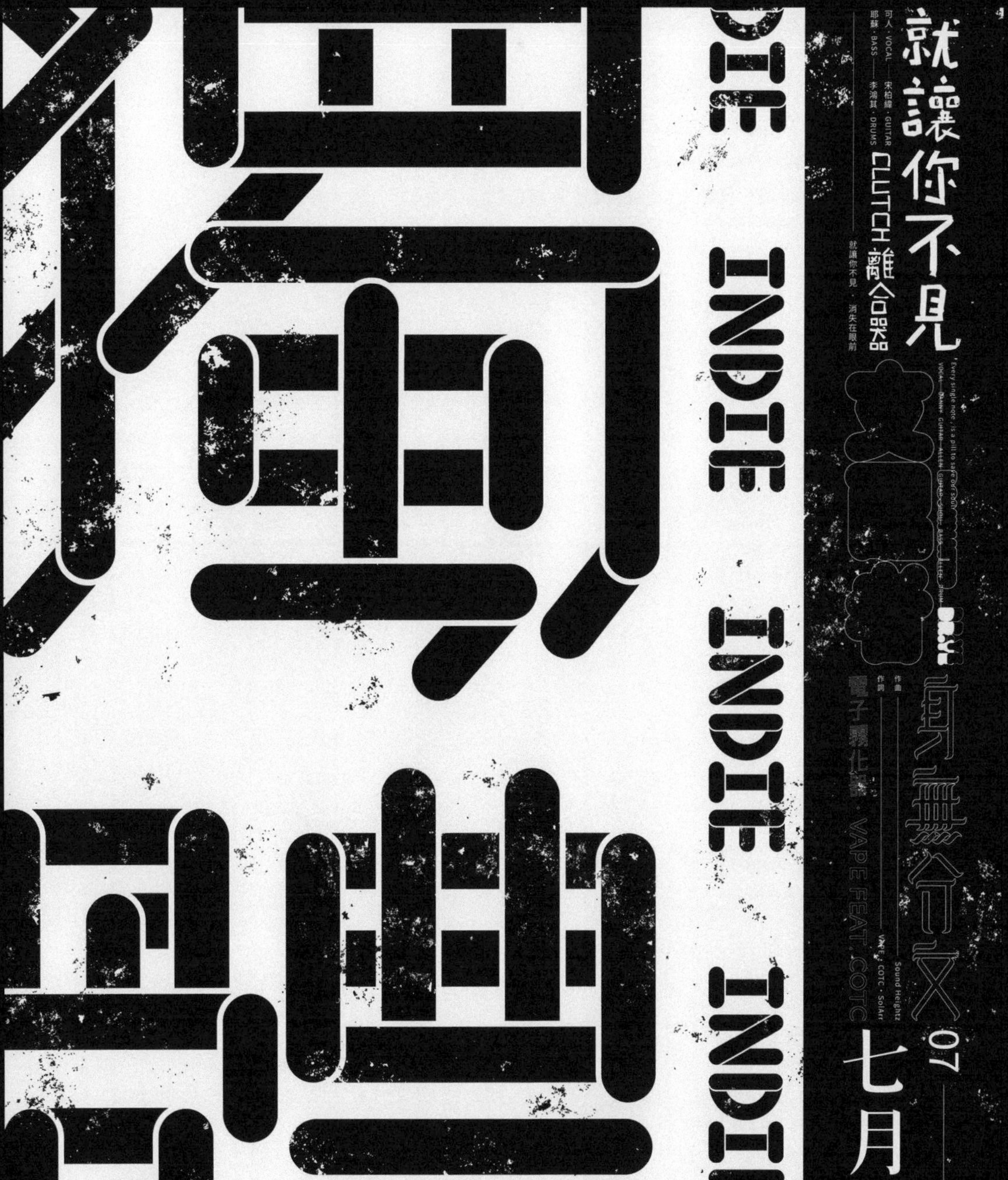

LETITIA LIN

042

Koviljka Neskovic, also known on socials as Hello This Is Kae is an Art Director currently based in Berlin. A child of the 80s, she was raised in Belgrade, studied in Venice and in the last 8 years worked in Italy, Serbia and also Germany.

Mega Spazio
(2018)

@kae._._._
www.hellothisiskae.com
www.behance.net/hellothisiskae

FES
TA
ESTATEEE
RITMO
RAGGIO
GIIIIRO
ACQUA
ONDA
SOLE
TRAMONTO
OMBRA

KAE X PTWSCHOOL 2018

Mega Spazio
(2018)

Mega Spazio is a space for communication and event production for music, design and art. From monthly music and design events to a festival development, it's based on a custom made typeface designed by Koviljka showcasing colourful visuals that transport you into a vibrant, colourful space.

Songs and the City
(2018)

In what began as a weekly Instagram project, Kovilijka would imagine classic 8Os and 9Os hits in the morning on her way to work and then, at the end of the day, come back home in the evening and transform them into something visual. Inspired by the cities and music videos viewed on **Youtube**, she created mockups that allowed people to live through the same experience as her, breathing the personality of the song and herself into each graphic. After posting them online, Kovilijka would return to the office the following day and find her colleagues singing them, which she happily joined in with.

Creative director, communication and graphic designer Tina Touli is a maker, speaker and educator. Tina currently runs her own London-based award-winning multidisciplinary studio, and also teaches at Central Saint Martins, University of the Arts London (UAL).

World Water Day Poster
(2017)

2017 marked the year of celebrating 3**0 years of Adobe Illustrator**. Tina produced a poster for this special anniversary designed during the **Graphic Design Adobe Live Stream**. Inspired by the way in which the pages of a book are turned, representing the past, the present and the future, a three dimensional paper sculpture was created and used as a guide for the design.

Another project Tina was involved in was titled **World Water Day**. A collection of five posters and a video was designed during the **Graphic Design Adobe Live Stream** in San Francisco, USA. The phrase "What about water? Watever, who cares!" has been used, calling the viewer to question his/her way of thinking towards the importance of water. In earlier experimentations, during a self initiated project in collaboration with Jakob Ritt and Yunxin Stella Wang, they came up with a technique where oil based and water based liquids were "mixed" to create interesting shapes and distortions that can be used for design outcomes. Inspired by these experimentations, a glass tray with oil and water has been placed on top of the typography in order to bring the water element to the project in a more unique and interesting way.

@tinatouli
www.tinatouli.com

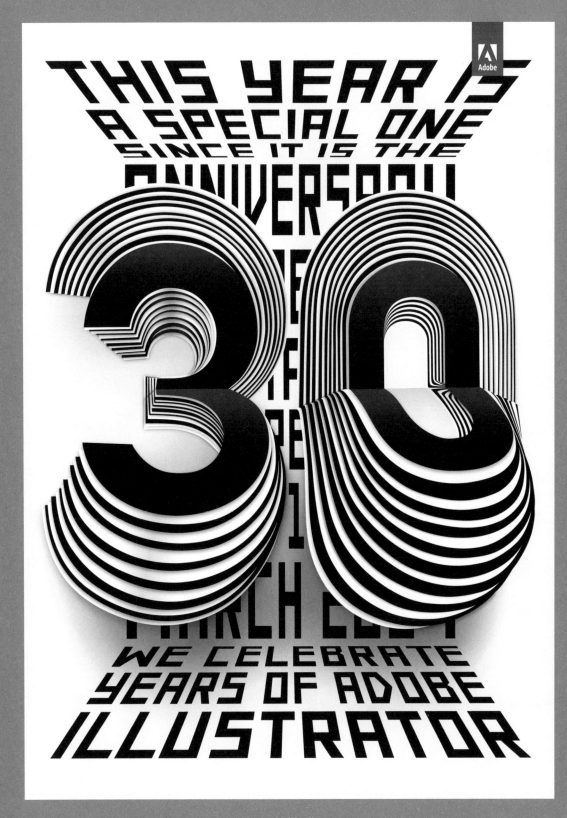

THIS YEAR IS A SPECIAL ONE SINCE IT IS THE ANNIVERSARY 30 WE CELEBRATE YEARS OF ADOBE ILLUSTRATOR

30 Years of Adobe Illustrator
(2017)

What will you do to tackle the water crisis? → 22nd of March ○ World Water Day

WHAT ABOUT WATER? WATEVER WHO CARES!

World Water Day ○ 22nd of March ← What will you do to tackle the water crisis?

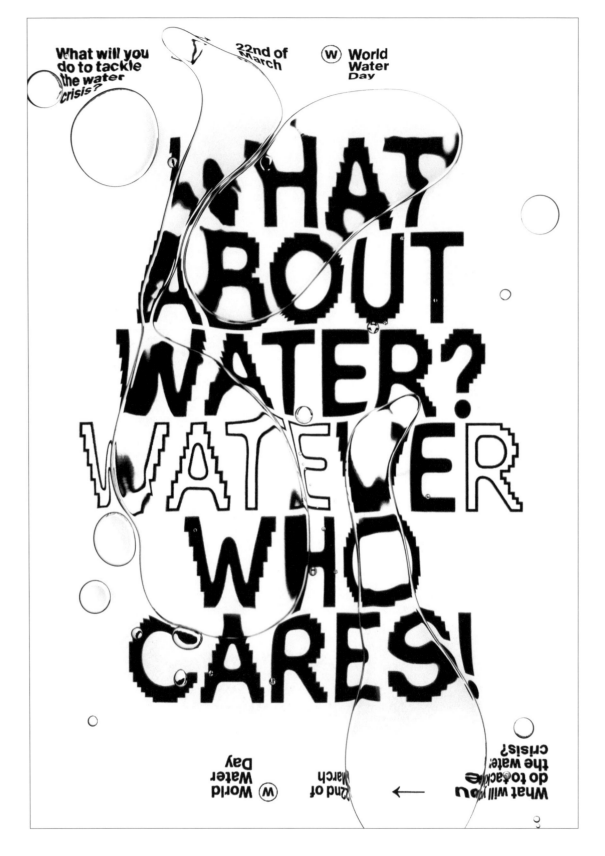

Anastasia is a Sydney, Australia-based graphic designer working across identity, campaign, web, dabbling in copywriting and most recently typeface design. With a background in both design and fine art much of Anastasia's work combines experimental processes with thoughtful and conceptually driven design solutions.

Bit Typeface Specimen
(2019)

anastasialiolio.com
@anastasialiolio

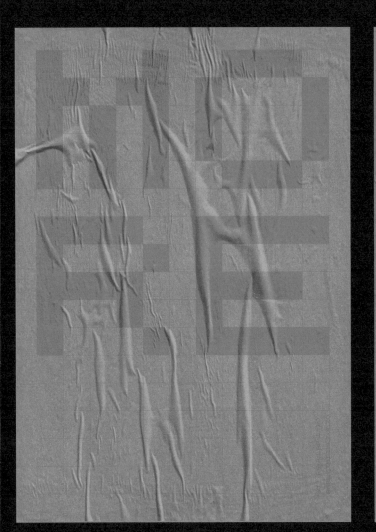
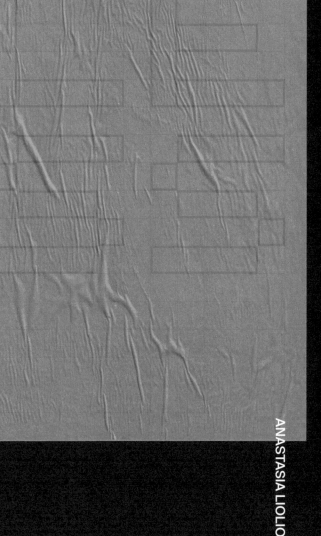

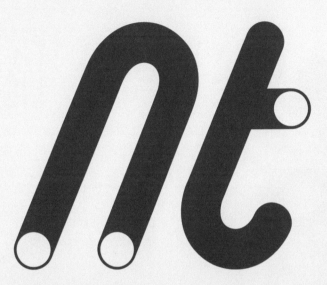

neon theory

ALYSSA CAVANAGH
PHOTOGRAPHER
NEONTHEORY.COM.AU
@NEONTHEORY

Project Q invites a diverse group of international thinkers and doers to apply next-wave thinking to the most pressing peace and security issues to their annually led Q Symposium. Scientists, humanists, diplomats, soldiers, and journalists engage chaos theory and quantum theory to explore observer-dependent events like natural disasters, regime change and diplomacy. The visual identity shows the complex and explorative nature of quantum theory. This included a dynamic logo and application of graphic elements to print and digital media.

Project Q
(2019)

With a special thanks to our listed supporters... —

ADE MILLS
ALEXANDRE MEIRELES MACHADO
ALEX NASSOUR
ANNE-CLAIRE PICKARD
ARCHIBALD KNESS
ARTURO ELENES
CIRCUS NETWORK
CHANDRA OSANN
CHLOE SHARP & NATASHA TOMALIN-HALL
CHRISTINA DIAS ANDRADE
VEDIA DESIGN — CLARA BRIONES VEDIA
DALY NETWORKS
DAN FORSTER
GRÁFICAS FIKA
HANNAH DAWSON
HARRY VINCENT
GREYJAM PRESS
IGNIO INNOVATION DESIGN
IGOR FRIDLAND
JAKE POLE
JEFFREY KALMIKOFF
JESSICA MÜLLER
KAI TALONPOIKA
KAREN T. CHEUNG
KRYSTYN HEIDE
KIMBERLY MAAS & DAVID POLITI

KRISTIN ROGERS BROWN
LAURA WHITEHOUSE
LILIAN FIGUEROA
LONDON SANS LTD
LUCIA RUSINAKOVA
LUKAS NOVOTNY
MANUAL FOUNDRY
MATTI BERG
NIGEL BALL
NEIL MCGUIRE
HELLO CREATIVE — NIKIE MARSTON
NIYLADESIGNS
OLIVIER TRÖNDLE
PETER PALLAND
QUIVER SUPPLY CO.
RIEMEA
RISO EAST PRINT STUDIO
ROBIN LAYFIELD
SADÉ OKAYLA ROACHE
SHANTI SPARROW
THE GARAGE PRESS — SIMON
SOMA STUDIO
SUZANNE PINDER
TIFFANY & JANE RABANAL-THREETS
TIMME LU
THE FAMILY
THE JAH CREATIONS — JUDITH HARVEY
TYPETURA
VAŠEK KOKEŠ
VILLAGE

INDEX

Typefaces

Type Projects

Name References

Processes